"This riveting first-hand narrative of th
2020 reminds us of what we've all lived
the history that will continue to haunt

Jeffrey C. H. Ngo, Geor

"Brian Kern's account is an absolute must-read for anyone interested in the 2019 protests. The brave people of Hong Kong put up fierce resistance against an oppressive regime, never backing down despite harsh reprisals. Their resilience and adaptability in the face of adversity are truly remarkable, and the book is a powerful reminder of their ongoing struggle at a time when the Chinese Communist Party seeks to erase Hong Kong's history."

Alex Chow, Umbrella Movement leader and Hong Kong diaspora activist

"As the Chinese Communist Party seeks to falsify Hong Kong's history, Brian Kern's book painstakingly preserves vivid snapshots of the city's shared memories. The world often speaks of the million-strong marches; this book reminds us of the lived experience of each of those millions, portraying their full humanity and heroism at this pivotal moment in Hong Kong history as they fight for the freedom and democracy that one day will be ours."

Anna Kwok, Executive Director, Hong Kong Democracy Council

"This is an extraordinarily comprehensive and interesting account of the demonstrations in Hong Kong in favour of that city's continued existence as a free society under the Rule of Law. The author provides a fascinating insider's look at what has happened which will be a defining issue for China's place in the twenty-first century."

Chris Patten, the last British governor of Hong Kong

"If you want to understand the raw mix of human emotions, frailties, soaring courage, definite weaknesses, real temptations and immense challenges that a struggle for freedom against tyranny entails, read this brilliant, captivating and inspiring book."

Benedict Rogers, founder and Chair of Hong Kong Watch

"An intimate, on-the-ground account that reveals the essence of the Hong Kong leaderless movement in 2019 – the robust social fabric that crystallis   one another –

First published in Asia by Mekong in 2020
Published in the United Kingdom by Bui Jones 2023

Copyright © Brian Kern

Brian Kern has asserted his right under the Copyright, Designs
and Patents Act 1988 to be identified as the author of this work

Cover photograph © Tyrone Sui/Reuters
Map illustrations by Katie Murphy

buijones.com
Bui Jones Limited Company Number 14823240

Printed and bound in Great Britain by Clays Ltd, Elcograf S.p.A.

A CIP catalogue record for this book is available from the British Library

ISBN 978-1-7394243-2-9

MIX
Paper from
responsible sources
FSC® C018072

All Bui Jones books are printed on
paper from responsible sources.

BRIAN KERN

Liberate Hong Kong

Stories from the Freedom Struggle

BUI JONES

It's not that we see hope and therefore we persist.
It's that through our persistence, hope is created.

– protest maxim

黎明來到要光復這香港
同行兒女為正義時代革命
祈求民主與自由萬世都不朽
我願榮光歸香港

The dawn has come. Liberate Hong Kong,
For justice, brothers and sisters, arm in arm, the revolution of our times.
Our quest for freedom and democracy will never falter.
May glory be to Hong Kong.

– last verse of the anthem "Glory to Hong Kong"

If we protect our hopes and devotion we persist
We light through our patience and broken resolve.

— Anna Akhmatova

黎明正向我们大地走来
向自由兄弟和姐妹们致意
不论任何时间的黑暗日子
民族和民主不会停不

The dawn has come. It salutes Hong Kong,
the freedom brothers and sisters, even so with the
revolution of all times.
With space for freedom and democracy will never
falter.

Mo ghrá sa tír a'bun

first verse of the ballad of liberty in Hong Kong.

To

the freedom fighters
for their determination, fortitude,
courage and creativity
in the pursuit of justice

all sisters and brothers in the struggle,
the 勇武 and the 和理非
for the unity and solidarity
that have made us a force to be reckoned with

all who have sacrificed and suffered
for the greater good
especially those whose lives were lost
as well as the arrested, prosecuted and seriously injured

the upstanding, generous people
who protected and sheltered my loved ones and me
when pursued by police and thugs

our children
who may not inherit the earth
but shall HK
for whatever that's worth

Y
for the shared struggle

in the hope that one day we shall all be free.

CONTENTS

Foreword   xiii

Preface   xxiii

The Battle of Lung Wo Road   1

Sanctuary   37

Running with the Kids   51

A Rioter   81

The Siege   117

Black Angels   159

See You at the Pot   209

A Timeline of the Hong Kong Protests   229

Names and identifying details have been changed. The freedom struggle goes on. Hong Kong is a city of masks. We look forward to the day when we can all remove them together.

FOREWORD

When *Liberate Hong Kong: Stories from the Freedom Struggle* was first published in 2020, the events it described were still a vivid memory for those who experienced it firsthand or who followed it closely from abroad, as I had done. The dramatic scenes in Hong Kong were long in the making; the frustration, but also the mistakable desperation of these actions, marked the end of a long road of over a decade of quiet diplomacy. The diverse people described as having made up the protest movement were recognisable. The context was well known, and framed how the protests were understood.

That a Chinese people felt compelled to reject Bejing's version of China and of the Chinese identity, and to see themselves as separate and oppressed people, was indicative of how poorly the authorities had played their hand. This was no longer a call for positive change, for the basic democratic rights Beijing had promised both the people of Hong Kong and the international community when the former British colony was handed to the People's Republic of China in 1997. The protests were rather about what type of city Hong Kong would be at its core. This is why universal suffrage mattered, as much a symbol of what Hong Kong should be as a demand to change how Hong Kong was governed. And if Hong Kong must change, it could not be said that Hong Kong did not go down without a fight.

"We are the proverbial frog slowly being boiled in a pot," I was often told a decade ago by those in civil society who were most sensitive to the changes. "We don't want to see what's happening, even as we feel the heat. And yet to the outside world nothing has changed."

The Hong Kong protests of 2019 were some of the largest, most creative and most sustained in history. At times more than a quarter of the population of the city were actively protesting. Despite the inconvenience and a ferocious disinformation campaign, the protesters continued to maintain the support of a majority of the city's residents, even as the protests grew more varied, more desperate and as violence escalated.

As increasingly graphic images were broadcast around the world, those outside the city or disconnected from those on the streets saw a city on fire fuelled by protesters and the police. Hong Kong was presented, not inaccurately, as a fight on the frontline between authoritarianism and freedom. But for Hongkongers, what we remembered most was that it did not begin this way.

What Hongkongers remember is the many years of failed engagement with a power that increasingly encroached on every aspect of our lives. A Chinese Communist Party that sought to shape our memories and rewrite our histories whilst demanding uncritical loyalty and love. We remember why the protests must be leaderless and tactics fluid – a lesson learnt from the crackdown that followed the 2014 protests, more popularly known as the Umbrella Movement. We also remember that peaceful protesters were labelled rioters at the start of the movement. When riotous behaviour was adopted by a minority of protesters, it was described as terrorism and the whole movement was condemned as a foreign plot. We noted that only companies with links to the Party, or who had spoken out against the protests, were targeted, and yet none were ever looted. We understood this not as the noble fight as there could never be victory, but as the final act of desperation of a people who had always asserted the right to remain true to themselves – a right that is intolerable to a totalitarian state.

Reading *Liberate Hong Kong* for the first time in 2020, I was glad that a view of the protests from one of the participants had been told with such knowledge, empathy and sensitivity. This was the people's story, told from the street.

Liberate Hong Kong is a valuable record of events from the perspective of Hongkongers who partook in the 2019 protests. It fills an important gap in public understanding, providing a sympathetic snapshot of the people who made up the more radical ends of the movement. It shines a light on the depth of feelings that spurred so many people to the streets, and provides answers to the more important questions arising from these protests: why did people feel compelled to act as they did?

These stories humanised an uprising that was too often dispassionately studied as yet another evolution of global dissent. The truth has always been that Hong Kong's circumstances are unique. It is the only former colony to have been handed over to an authoritarian state, and the only instance of a people being denied a say in the process of decolonisation. It raises uncomfortable questions about how we have chosen to remember colonialism – there were, and are, more oppressive and less just forms of government. It also shows us how a free, open and liberal society may be undermined, foreshadowing the challenges a rising China and ever greater Chinese influence pose around the world.

Reading *Liberate Hong Kong* today I am acutely aware of how differently I responded to the book. Whilst it has lost none of its value as a powerful documentation of the people, personalities and motivations of those who took to the street, the passage of time has highlighted just how much and how quickly Hong Kong has changed, and also how much my own memories of small, yet key, details of what defined the nature of these protests had faded – and how into these spaces a new narrative is taking root. This is especially the case in Hong Kong.

Hong Kong today is a city changed. A friend who was recently there summed up these changes when he told me how within the first few days of being back in the city he had seriously contemplated buying a home there. "Superficially, Hong Kong remains a truly beautiful city and a great place to be." Yes, it had changed, but if you kept your head down and avoided politics you could still live there quite happily. It is still very different from mainland China – which remains true.

Yet as the weeks went by and he and his family returned

to old haunts and caught up with old friends, the veil began to drop. The facade could no longer disguise a city that had lost its soul, and that could only exist, at least officially, within a lie.

"The more people we spoke to, the more depressed we became." Some people existed in a state of self-delusion, believing in whatever would justify their confidence in a city that privileged them in a way no other city could. In others, a part of them had died. Conversations had changed or ended completely.

"What's the point of talking about anything serious? What's the point of having aspirations?" The powerless had learnt to feel their powerlessness very acutely. Always pragmatic, Hong Kong has discovered that the meaning of pragmatism had changed.

Every person has been affected. Everyone is related to or knows someone who has been caught up in the crackdowns. Lifelong friendships have been erased from memory. Families have been divided. People have turned to trivial pursuits, as far away from any imagined political red lines. An interest in gardening is booming among the social elite.

It is not simply a matter of avoiding politics, or knowing where the red lines lie. Just beneath the surface there are deep wounds in society that cannot be acknowledged, and they slowly fester. An information environment, whilst retaining the pretense of being open, is now heavily aligned with the political narrative in Beijing. Once the gateway to China, Hong Kong today is a global gateway for Chinese Communist Party influence.

My friend left after six weeks. He did not buy a property. His view of the city had worsened. "If this is the last time that I visit Hong Kong I would not care," he said, even though this would mean leaving behind family and a business. To de-politicise a society is itself a most political of acts: for it is politics that now defines where the red lines are drawn – and, perhaps most worryingly, how far the rule of law still carries. Over 30 years in Hong Kong and China taught him that these things matter.

Once a refuge from political persecution, today hundreds of thousands of Hongkongers have fled their homes. Hundreds more have applied for political asylum abroad. The core of what was once a thriving civil society has been gutted. International NGOs have left the city. Independent trade unions have closed. Journalists, lawyers and teachers have fled the city in large numbers. The Hong Kong described in the book was a city fighting to continue to be able to speak truth to power. Today, that fight has ended. The preservation of truth has moved overseas.

In January 2023 the US government recognised over 1,200 political prisoners in the city. Six months later the figure is closer to 1,600. Among them are many of the city's leading lawyers, academics and former legislators – people of international standing. Many more are prevented from leaving the city. And as in China, families are being used to silence dissent.

The places remain, but the Hong Kong of *Liberate Hong Kong* is over. The people we meet in the book were a people captured at a specific moment in time. For all that we may wish, that time has gone. Not even desperation remains. The flame of hope burns dimly out of sight.

As Beijing understands it, Hong Kong has been "harmonised" and "stability" has returned. New and patriotic residents are learning the "correct" history, and learning to love the motherland – and hate the West. In local schools the talking points of Chinese-styled national and patriotic education are being promoted at school. Primary school children are being taught about the Opium Wars, to feel the Century of Humiliation, and to let this frame their understanding. Parents dare not challenge this for fear of being reported.

Returning to *Liberate Hong Kong* brought home not only how much Hong Kong had changed, but also how my own recollections and judgements had shifted. As memories fade, a new narrative slips in to fill the void, reshaping the way we remember.

This manipulation of memory has been quite deliberate. The Chinese Communist Party have consistently rewritten and used history to legitimise their rule. For an opaque and undemocratic regime, such legitimacy matters. It is also a legitimacy that they can control.

As with Taiwan today, Hong Kong once offered the world a tantalising glimpse of what China might be if it were free, open and liberal. It provided a Chinese alternative to a Chinese one-party state – an alternative understanding of what China was, is and could be. It represented a different relationship with Chinese history, and of a proud and rejuvenated Chinese future; and that China could be more than a Communist People's Republic with Chinese characteristics, but a free and open (and democratic) nation. China was not the Chinese Communist Party, nor did the Party define what it means to be Chinese. This was the challenge.

I first met Brian Kern in early 2014. Unlike some others who, as expatriates, had the privilege of choosing Hong Kong as home, Brian wanted to know what was happening in society and on the street. He saw Hong Kong as a true Hongkonger, as much more than a place, but as a home and, importantly, as a home to a people. He understood the value of civil society both as an expression of the freedoms that defined this city, and as a way to shape the type of city that was Hong Kong's promise.

That Brian had long published under a pen name, Kong Tsung-gan, was known by those who followed events in Hong Kong. A pen name was understandable, given that activists and those associated with the protests were regularly doxxed. This was encouraged by leading pro-China voices, including Hong Kong's former leader. He was also known and popular with journalists, given his close personal relationships with many of those most active in the protest movement. It helped that he is fluent in English and a gifted writer.

Brian and his family no longer live in Hong Kong. For his association with the protest movement, for using a pen name and for being an American, he has been accused of being a foreign agent. Despite his clear love for the Hong Kong people, he has also been accused of being a racist. Propagandists understand the power of these terms. In the Hong Kong I knew, these lies might be challenged and exposed for what they are. However these lies are foundational to the new Hong Kong; and over time, these lies, even if we do not believe them at first, slip in to our unconscious, shaping and distorting the way we remember and understand.

Within three years I, like so many Hongkongers, have seen close friends and family change in ways that are both deeply disappointing but also frightening. My former school principal, a Briton now retired in Hong Kong, today writes regularly for Chinese state-media, softly pushing Chinese Communist Party talking points. He declares there are no political prisoners in Hong Kong, nor that any Hongkongers are in exile. What, I wonder, would he say to former students currently seeking political asylum abroad?

To survive in the new Hong Kong, one doesn't necessarily have to believe the lie in full. However, to maintain a clear conscience, you must be willing to reject the truth, which is that Hong Kong today is a moral question. No one in Hong Kong is unaffected. Almost every family knows someone who has suffered. No longer free to speak out and to stand by the accused, people are choosing to forget.

Like Brian, I and my family have had to leave. We are but two of many who were hounded out of our homes. We have been joined by hundreds of thousands of others. What we all share in common was that we loved Hong Kong for what it was, not for what Beijing has determined it to be.

Evan Fowler

PREFACE

This is my third book on Hong Kong. The first book, *Umbrella: A Political Tale from Hong Kong*, is an exhaustive 600-page history of the Umbrella Movement that one reader described as "exhausting". The second book came out in March 2019, just months before the protests. It's called *As long as there is resistance, there is hope: Essays on the Hong Kong freedom struggle in the post-Umbrella Movement era, 2014–2018*. It tracks the major political developments in Hong Kong after the Umbrella Movement, in particular the many ways in which the Chinese Communist Party attempted to gain greater control, and brings the history of the city up to the moment.

When I contemplated writing about the protests, they seemed too huge, a magnitude greater than the Umbrella Movement. The only way I could figure to get a handle on them was to write about the events I have experienced, the people I have known. The book is not all-encompassing or encyclopaedic, as *Umbrella* might be, but I hope it captures both the spirit of the protests and the many different aspects of a multifaceted movement.

The title of this book, *Liberate Hong Kong*, is one of the key protest slogans. The full slogan is "liberate Hong Kong, revolution of our times". Eight Chinese characters: 光復香港時代革命. It embodies the spirit of the protests. It can be seen and heard all over Hong Kong, scrawled in graffiti on walls, in white on black flags, chanted over and over again at every protest. Ever present, it echoes in your ears.

It was first coined by Edward Leung Tin-kei in 2016. Leung was one of the young new leaders to emerge in the post-Umbrella era. He was the head of Hong Kong Indigenous, the most influential localist group. At the time, the slogan didn't travel far. On the first day of Chinese New Year in February 2016, police and protesters clashed in the streets of Mong Kok through the night. They were the most violent altercations between police and citizens in Hong Kong since the Cultural Revolution-inspired leftist riots of the late 1960s. Leung and several dozen others were put on trial for "riot" and convicted. He was sentenced to six years in prison, one of the longest protest-related sentences ever in Hong Kong. Prison is where he has been during the protests and where he remains now. In 2016, Leung was considered by many a divisive figure. It would have been hard to imagine the so-called peaceful, rational protesters, especially those from the traditional pro-democracy parties, shouting his slogan out in the streets in 2019, spilling into 2020. That it has come to this is a sign of just how unified all of the factions of the freedom struggle have become, as well as of the power of the slogan's words.

The word "liberate" in the slogan can also be translated as "reclaim". In Chinese, it's 光復, which literally means "reclaim the light". It has a strongly revolutionary air dating to the time of republican efforts to overthrow the Qing dynasty at the turn of the twentieth century. That's when the phrase was first used to connote political liberation. Of course, the fact would not have been missed by the Chinese Communist Party that many of those early republicans, including Sun Yat-sen, often regarded as the father of modern China, used the safe harbour of British colonial Hong Kong to launch the revolution. The fact that the Party and its Hong Kong puppet government felt compelled to attack the slogan showed just how spooked they are, for, after all, they're Qing redux, the next dynasty ripe for overthrowing.

The subtitle of the book is *Stories from the Freedom Struggle*. That is what follows. Each story stands alone. Some overlap. The focus of the stories reflects the leaderless ethos of the movement. None of the people who appear are prominent or well known. The stories attempt to evoke the experience, the lived texture of the struggle. They're not centred on key events of the protests. Rather, those events emerge in the course of telling about the characters' lives. I've written the stories in the midst of the protests, while they are still going on. It's been difficult to find the time to write. I often felt so uncalm and upset that it took considerable will and discipline to settle down enough to concentrate. The stories were written fast and under intense and distracting circumstances. They emerged from scribbled notes and experiences that had just occurred.

Thanks to publisher and editor Minh Bui Jones for the opportunity to write this book and share it with the world and for his affirming belief in the historical importance of the Hong Kong freedom struggle.

Thanks as well to Tom Grundy, who published an earlier version of "Sanctuary" in *Hong Kong Free Press*.

Liberate Hong Kong, revolution of our times!

CENTRAL HONG KONG

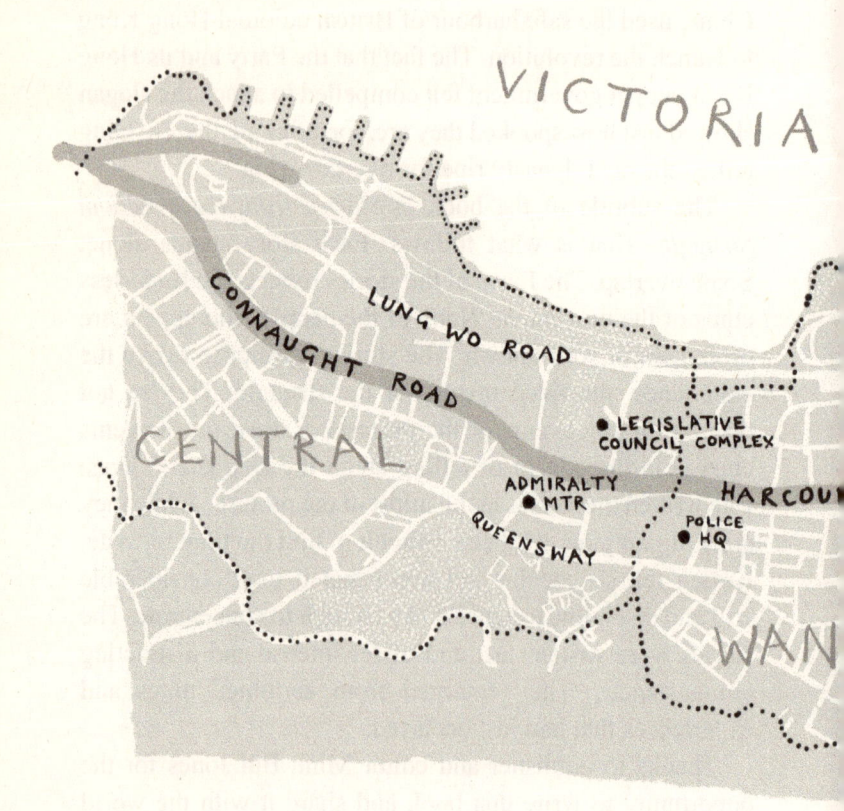

VICTORIA

LUNG WO ROAD

CONNAUGHT ROAD

CENTRAL

● LEGISLATIVE COUNCIL COMPLEX

ADMIRALTY
● MTR

QUEENSWAY

HARCOUR

● POLICE HQ

WAN

HARBOUR

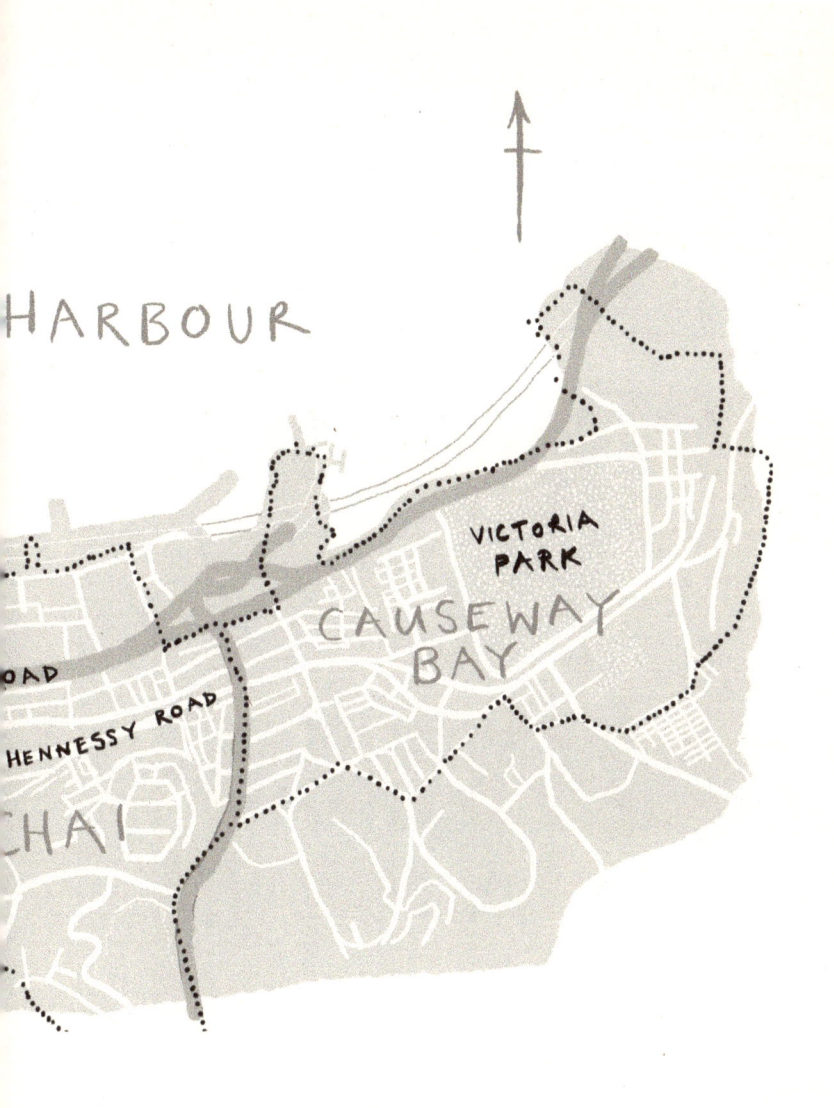

VICTORIA PARK

CAUSEWAY BAY

HENNESSY ROAD

CHAI

KOWLOON

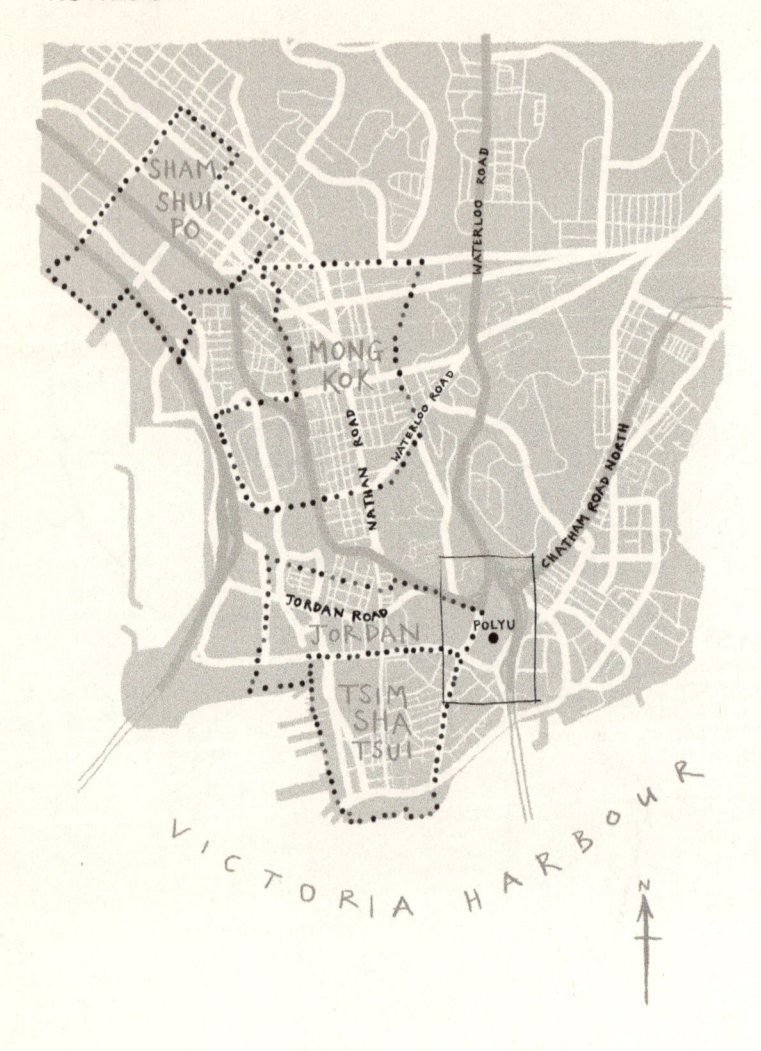

POLYU CAMPUS

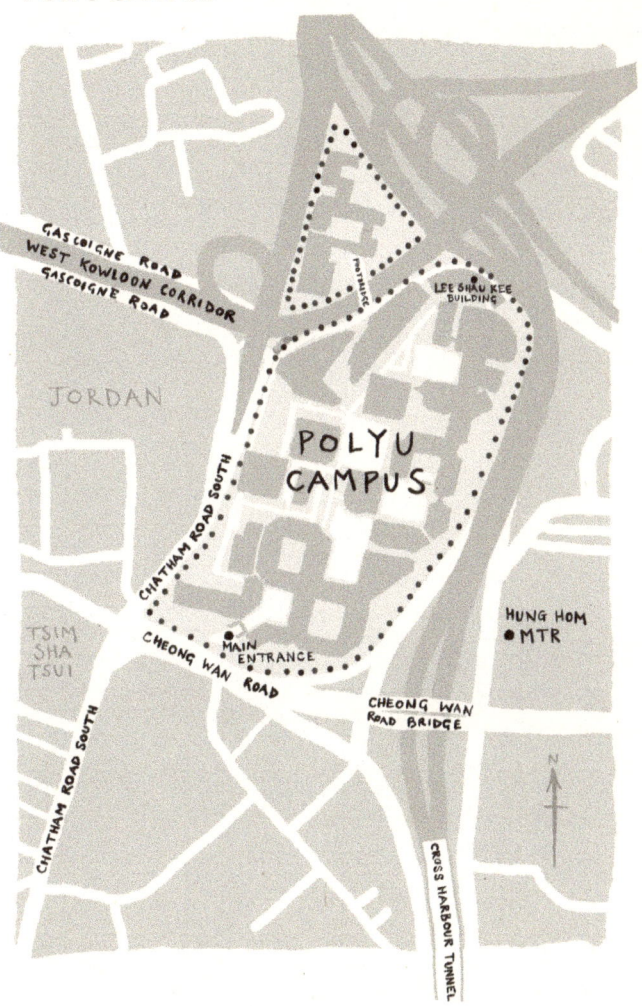

THE BATTLE OF LUNG WO ROAD

是你教我們和平遊行是沒用的

It is you who taught us that peaceful protests
do not work

*– graffiti by protesters on a column in the
Legislative Council building, 1 July 2019*

I met Francis through Nancy. It was at the memorial march for Liu Xiaobo.

That's how I remember when we met. Xiaobo died on 13 July 2017. The march was a couple of days after that, right before Nancy was diagnosed with ovarian cancer.

Francis was much younger. Nancy and I had been involved in the freedom struggle for years. To us, Xiaobo's death seemed like the end of an era.

Nancy said she and Francis had gotten to know each

other when they both were arrested at the Battle of Lung Wo Road. That was during the Umbrella Movement. When police charged, they sat on the ground, old non-violent civil resistance style. Most of the others ran away. The police couldn't catch anyone else, so they arrested Francis and Nancy and a few others. The two struck up a conversation in the police van on the way to jail, whispering to each other as the cops shouted at them to remain silent.

They were both charged with obstructing police. All they'd been doing was sitting on the ground. They didn't actively or intentionally impede police in carrying out their action. Police could easily go around them.

Francis accepted a prosecution offer to bind him over: in exchange for the prosecution not pursuing the charge to a full trial and potential conviction, Francis had to promise not to commit a similar public order offence for the next year.

For Nancy, it was a matter of principle: she was convicted and appealed all the way to the High Court. Where she lost. She was fined a few thousand Hong Kong dollars. The whole legal process had taken years. In fact, it had just finished. I knew what that kind of infinity trial was like. It hung over your life. Even if you faced it with equanimity, as Nancy did, it was gruelling.

And just as it finished, she was diagnosed with cancer. I joked she had gotten it to show solidarity with Xiaobo.

"Ha ha funny," she said. "Just hope I don't end up like him."

Francis had been listening to Nancy's story of how they'd met. He chuckled. "You won't catch me doing that again."

"What?"

"That non-violent civil disobedience crap."

We were way at the back of the march. Unusual for me.

I liked to be at the front, to see what was coming. It was the evening of an intensely hot day. Sweat poured down marchers' foreheads, glistening in the light from the street lamps. We all held candles in two hands out in front of us on the way to the Liaison Office, the entity set up by the Chinese Communist Party (CCP) to "liaise" with Hong Kong, though it would be more accurate to say that its purpose was to control; it was the centre of evil, the city's dark heart. The marchers wished to lay the blame for Xiaobo's death in custody at the regime's doorstep. The police were waiting for us there.

Francis was a non-stop talker. He talked so much I feared it might seem a bit disrespectful of the solemnity of the occasion. He seemed oblivious of his surroundings. But then I thought, Xiaobo was a talker, he loved to engage in debate, he was a man of words, he'd consider Francis's iconoclastic nonchalance a tribute.

He was one of the few young people on the march. Most of us were veterans, had been coming to protests like this for years. And, in the eyes of young people like Francis, hadn't made any progress at all. I'd hoped for a better turnout. There were a few thousand; not bad, but it was the sort of thing I thought all of Hong Kong should turn out for. The Party had just killed a Nobel Peace Prize laureate after all.

Francis said, "I don't usually go to stuff like this. But he's a pretty good guy. He stood up to the Commies. He never gave in and he never gave up. I respect him for that." He added, "I couldn't care less about China. I don't want anything to do with it. But I hate the Commies. I'll fight them to the death."

It had already been nearly three years since the Umbrella Movement, in response to which the Party had gone on the offensive, seeking to gain greater control over Hong Kong and assimilate it. With each step it took, I wondered, when are Hong Kong people going to fight back? They reminded me of a guy getting shoved over and over by a bully. Which shove would finally trigger a response?

The post-Umbrella years had seen the rise of localism, especially among young people. Its basic idea: the necessity of defending Hong Kong against Party attempts to gobble it up. Localists often regarded the older generation with disdain for its failure to do just that and for its naivety about communism.

Francis was a university student. I asked him how things were there. He said, "In my faculty, there's no debate on whether you're for or against the government; everyone's against. The only debate is whether the struggle should remain non-violent or not."

"What about the debate on whether or not one should be involved in the struggle?"

"What do you mean?"

"Just that it seems like, since the Umbrella Movement, a lot of young people have checked out."

"We'll be back," he assured me. "We'll be back."

"I hope so. We need you," I said, looking at all the middle-aged faces around us. "But I'm beginning to wonder."

✷

After that, I saw Francis occasionally. We liked to go to Hong Kong national team football matches and boo the anthem of the People's Republic of China (PRC), something that had become a tradition going back to 2015. FIFA fined the Hong Kong Football Association, but the fans kept right on booing. The association was the only one ever fined for fans booing what was supposed to be their own anthem. But that was the point: it wasn't, and we didn't want it. To us, it was a symbol of colonial oppression. If we had our own national team, why not our own national anthem?

To retaliate, the Chinese Communist Party passed a new law in the PRC against insulting or disrespecting the anthem, a law entirely unnecessary since there'd never been a single reported case of people in the PRC doing anything like that (and even if there had been, no such laws should exist). But the Party needed to do that in order to then insert it into the Hong Kong Basic Law, as its real intention was to criminalise insulting the anthem in Hong Kong.

Once the CCP did that, Francis and I got the crowd defiantly chanting, "We'll all be going to prison soon, we'll all be going to prison soon", just after booing the anthem once again. We were tickled at the prospect of the police trying to cart thousands of fans off to prison. Prison was the Party's answer to everything, and it was becoming Hong Kong's too.

Sometimes he introduced me to his friends. I spent a lot of time in those post-Umbrella years arguing with young people. There was no reason to be depressed about the outcome of the Umbrella Movement. The movement was actually a great success: it had ensured that the CCP's fake suffrage stood no chance of passage. We'd defended Hong Kong. The freedom struggle was long term. The future depended on them; the young people who saw Hong Kong's situation more clearly than most had no illusions about the Party and wanted nothing to do with a China under CCP rule. "You're the whole foundation of our long-term resistance."

What I liked about Francis was, he had the fighting spirit. I knew he would never stop fighting. Like Xiaobo. You could build a movement out of people like him.

Whenever I saw him, he'd talk about his latest research into armed uprisings. He was nothing if not an assiduous student. One discussion would be about ETA, the Basque separatists. Francis argued their armed approach was more effective than the non-violence of the Catalans in achieving concrete gains towards greater autonomy. Another time, it would be the Irish Republican Army (IRA).

Francis, I believed, romanticised these armed movements. I told him while I supported the republican cause, and could even countenance some forms of violence targeting security forces, I felt it was important to denounce the IRA's targeting of civilians and its acts of terrorism, not to mention the various ways in which it intimidated and bullied its own people.

Francis even expressed admiration for ISIS. "Honestly, I hate them for what they've done, but what I admire is their determination, their courage, their willingness to die for their cause." He felt something similar was needed in Hong Kong and also thought that, when the time for armed struggle came, the Middle East was a natural source of weapons.

In response, I cited a study by the political scientist Erica Chenoweth comparing non-violent and violent resistance movements in the twentieth century. It showed that non-violent ones were significantly more successful. From a strictly strategic perspective, from the point of view of efficacy, you were better off being non-violent.

Francis scoffed at my arguments. "You can give me all the evidence you want," he said, "but what evidence do you have from HK? We've been fighting non-violently for years, and where has it got us? Yeah, we've managed to block a few bad things from happening, but we're no closer to achieving any of our positive goals. So you can stick that non-violence bullshit up your ass. It's so yesterday."

The victories Francis was referring to were against the introduction of draconian security legislation (named Article 23 after the article in the Basic Law that supposedly required Hong Kong to enact laws on "national security") in 2003 that many feared would erode our civil liberties; the introduction of a new school subject called Moral and National Education that many considered a form of Communist brainwashing in 2012; and the fake suffrage proposal of 2015. All were significant victories, and the only examples of anyone under its rule standing up to the Party and winning, but they were defensive actions, to prevent the worst from happening.

So Francis was quite correct that we had made no significant positive gains. In fact, during all our years of non-violent struggle, the CCP was gaining a tighter grip over the city, eroding our already compromised autonomy and rights.

What could I say then to his argument except, Well, you've just got to keep fighting, it's a long-term struggle, etc. etc.? I couldn't blame the youth for their impatience – and I took their talk of armed struggle as primarily an expression of that impatience. Indeed, if anything, I thought it a positive attribute: greater impatience was required of the older generations.

"You won't find me ever again sitting out in the road doing nothing when the police charge," Francis said. "I was arrested at the Battle of Lung Wo Road even though I didn't fight." He scoffed, "Hah! We call it a battle, but we didn't even fight. Next time, I'll give them a good reason to arrest me. Next time, I fight back."

*

When the protests came along, we'd been out of touch for some time. But I thought of Francis, especially on 12 June.

Three days earlier, on the 9th, more than a million people had come out to protest against the extradition bill. Even while the march was still going, the government issued a statement saying it was going ahead with the bill, rejecting the demand of the marchers, who made up one-seventh of the entire Hong Kong population. As I read the statement, shaking my head, Francis's voice echoed: Where has non-violence ever got us?

The plan on the 12th was to get out early and surround the Legislative Council (Legco) building before the pro-Communist representatives had a chance to arrive. The bill was scheduled for debate that day. The government wanted it passed via an expedited process. The rigged, pro-Communist-dominated Legco planned to oblige by doing so within a matter of days.

Starting early that morning, thousands streamed towards government headquarters, turning into tens of thousands as the morning went on. Almost all were young people. My heart leapt. For five years, ever since the Umbrella Movement, I'd been waiting for these young people, and now here they were.

I wanted to shout, So good to see you! Where have you all been? and hug every one of them. But I was one of the few elated: the mood was grim, purposeful, businesslike: we were there to get something done, not to celebrate their return to the streets.

And accomplish something we did: by mid-morning, the Legco session for the day would be cancelled. The next day's session would be as well. In less than three weeks, young protesters would break into Legco and briefly occupy it. The full Legislative Council would end up not meeting again until October, by which time the political landscape had radically changed from what it was on that morning of the 12th.

But now that they were out, accomplishing their first task, blocking Legco from meeting, wasn't enough: they were pushing for the withdrawal of the bill. And they set a deadline: 3pm that day. If the deadline wasn't met, there would be an escalation.

I was alarmed when I heard that: What would the escalation be? Wasn't that bad timing? Shouldn't we at least wait until people got off work? Then, even more would come out and we'd have greater safety in numbers.

The government headquarters was well fortified and you could just feel the police straining at the leash. Some stood behind their barricades taunting and mocking us, wielding their weapons threateningly, pointing guns at us, as if they just couldn't wait to use them.

Their lesson from the Umbrella Movement was that they hadn't been tough enough: you couldn't just let people camp out in the streets for 79 days, you had to stop these things from even happening and not allow protesters a chance to entrench themselves, and you had to do so with overwhelming force. Towards that end, the government had opened its coffers and showered police with abundant "crowd control" equipment. The hardliners within the force were the ones who'd received promotions and were in the key operational decision-making positions. I had no illusions about the police's plans.

There were rumours that protesters were digging up bricks from the pavement. I went around looking for any signs of that, but could find none. (Elsewhere, as it turned out, some had taken bricks from a nearby construction site; not many, but a few.) I also tried to persuade anyone I could not to escalate, at least not so early. It was on that day that the trope of the "leaderless movement" was born, and leaderless it was: the call to escalate had gone out anonymously online, there was no face I could speak to.

Three o'clock came and sure enough: hard hats, umbrellas and plastic water bottles began to fly. Where I was, only a few dozen protesters were throwing these objects at the police. In another location, there'd been bricks and metal poles as well.

At this point, there were easily 100,000 people out on the street, the vast majority young. Oh, shit, I thought, we've handed the police their perfect pretext on a platter.

And sure enough: police wasted no time. Not only did they go after the dozens throwing objects at them, they attacked us all, all 100,000 of us.

They shot tear gas for the first time since the beginning of the Umbrella Movement on 28 September 2014 and followed it up with rubber bullets and sponge grenades. (Eventually, that day, 240 rounds of tear gas, 19 rubber bullets, three beanbag rounds and 23 sponge grenades, to be precise, would be shot).

They pushed us away from government headquarters and in what seemed an incredibly short time, managed to disperse us all. It felt like a defeat. I was dejected: we had government headquarters surrounded and we lost it.

It was only over the next 24 hours that I began to realise what had occurred: in employing all of their might, in bringing all of their "less lethal" force to bear on us, the police had achieved a "military" victory – their objective of clearing the protesters was met – but scored an enormous own goal: throughout Hong Kong and all over the world, the images transmitted were those of tear gas and police abuses.

And they were suckered into the attack by those few dozen protesters who'd escalated by throwing stuff at them. Who says "violence" doesn't work? In fact, that day, it worked remarkably well. Arguably, it took an immense but potentially one-off million-person-march and turned it into a movement.

What happened on the 12th was the beginning of a pattern that would play itself out again and over during the protests: police overreaction accomplished its immediate mission but provoked a stronger counter-reaction, from protesters, from ordinary citizens; the movement gained momentum, opposition to police brutality grew.

And it was as if the police simply couldn't help themselves: once they purchased all that crowd control equipment, the overwhelming temptation was to use it; once they'd promoted all those hardliners to key decision-making positions, it was as if their decisions were almost predetermined.

Who knows what those escalators intended on 12 June, but they succeeded. That was the beginning of me thinking maybe I didn't know everything there was to know about effective protest, the beginning of my disorientation. Who needed to "hold territory" anyway? That was outmoded Umbrella Movement thinking. Be water. Move. Flow. Play to your strengths.

Just how well did "violence" work? On 9 June, even while more than a million marched, the government rejected our demands. On 15 June, three days after the surrounding of government headquarters and while the fallout from the police attack was still occurring, the chief executive, the top leader of Hong Kong, announced she was "suspending" the extradition bill. Listen to a million non-violent protesters? No way. A few dozen protesters throw stuff, police massively overreact, and suddenly the bill is "suspended".

The chief executive, Carrie Lam, was hoping to halt the momentum building towards the next day's march, to placate and pacify the masses. Most of the media, after the announcement of the bill's suspension, assumed she had. After all, hadn't she given the protesters what they wanted? But the media didn't quite understand what was going on in Hong Kong. Maybe no one did. It was impossible to predict the enormous scale of the protest.

The next day, two million marched, just a week after a million had. The whole city was in revolt. The floodgates had opened. It was about much more than the extradition bill now.

*

Following the blowback against their aggression on 12 June, the police were ordered to back off. It was a necessary public relations ploy. The same dynamic had occurred in the Umbrella Movement: first the police attacked citizens with tear gas for eight hours, then they entirely disappeared from the streets and ceded the occupied areas to protesters for months. This time, the retreat and passivity on the part of the police would continue until after protesters broke into the Legco building on 1 July. At that point, they saw it didn't work; we were just taking advantage of it. And they swung way back in the other direction: crackdown, tough talk, calling the protests riots. But that was still a couple weeks off.

First we besieged their headquarters.

On 21 June, five days after the two-million-person march, I was outside Legco, now about to be closed early for summer recess due to the protests, wondering if anything would happen. There were a few hundred gathered there, but not much going on and no plan. As so often during the protests, I was afraid that people would just give up, that the protests would stop. When people see videos of protests, they think they're exciting, but really, as a protester, you spend a lot of your time just waiting around. Most of the time, nothing happens – and then, something does.

I passed a leader of one of the groups I thought might be planning something and asked, "What's up? Anything happening?"

He kept walking right on past and muttered under his breath, "Might go to the police station." An hour or so after that, people went out into Harcourt Road, the busy thoroughfare flanking government headquarters. A road occupation, then. As had occurred time and again in the past, first and foremost during the Umbrella Movement, but as recently as the night after the two-million-person march. You could almost hear the multilane highway groan, I've been occupied so often. Isn't it enough?

But as I watched a few dozen protesters drag barriers out into the road, I noticed a kind of procession occurring, farther up the road, crossing it and heading eastward, momentarily escaping the attention of all of the media cameras gathered there, waiting for something to happen, just like me.

Aha, I thought. They *are* going there.

By the time I caught up with them, thousands had gathered at police headquarters. From the steps leading up to the main entrance, Joshua Wong spoke. He'd just got out of prison a few days before, having served a sentence related to the Umbrella Movement, and his presence there that day would get him arrested more than two months later, on 30 August, along with Demosistō party fellows Agnes Chow and Ivan Lam, for inciting, organising and participating in an unlawful assembly. On that day, however, 21 June, the police, in front of whose house we stood and whose legal power it was to declare an assembly unlawful, never told us we were unlawfully assembled.

As word got out we'd gone to the HQ, the crowd swelled into the tens of thousands and managed to surround the enormous compound covering a whole city block. They got to work almost immediately. Entrances were barricaded. The façade and compound were covered in graffiti. "Fuck the Popo" went up right below the Police Headquarters sign. It later became the title and refrain of a smash-hit rap song heard everywhere, garnering upwards of two million views online, as well as a common protest slogan. Security cameras were smashed and spray-painted.

The police did nothing. From a glass-covered walkway high above that linked two towers of the complex, senior officers looked down, mere spectators of the vandalism of the building under their command. One entrance to the compound was left open for civilians who worked for the police to evacuate. Over the course of the afternoon, hundreds streamed out. Wow, I thought, so many work inside there. Aside from those civilians, there were in fact more than 30,000 police officers, the most over-resourced public institution in a city with one of the lowest crime rates in the world. All to be prepared precisely for times such as these, when you had to keep the rabble down. And now those 30,000 officers, who'd attacked us only nine days before, could do nothing but watch. You could nearly feel emanating through the walls the frustration at their political masters telling them to stand down. All I could think was, sooner or later we're going to be made to pay for this.

It was a festival of rage. One journalist said he felt as if he were witnessing a medieval purging ritual, a mass exorcism. On 12 June, I thought of those thousands of young people who suddenly emerged from underground at Legco like rats coming out of the sewers. On 21 June, the protesters were like ants, swarming over everything, going about the business of destruction. They wanted to tear everything apart. If you believed that a public institution must retain the public's trust in order to have any legitimacy, you saw the police force as a public institution ending that day before your very eyes.

Towards nightfall, eggs started flying, just a few to begin with, then a deluge, crashing against the façade of the station where "Fuck the Popo" had been sprayed hours before, the clear gelatinous contents creating dark patterns as they dribbled down the grey stone.

For a reason that was hard to fathom, while all police had withdrawn into the main building and compound, a small group of between five and ten remained stationed outside, behind a parapet at the top of an escalator, about 10 metres off the ground. They stood in front of a metal shutter that had long ago been pulled down. Inevitably, they were the ones who became the primary target of the eggs.

It took a good shot to throw it both that high and far. Ones that fell short crashed against the building's façade. But after a few throws, many found their range. It became like target practice. Several dozen chucked the eggs while thousands others looked on, cheering whenever the target was hit. You could hear the *crack splat crack* of the eggs crashing against the body-length plastic transparent shields the officers held to protect themselves. They were getting pelted. Eggs rained down on them.

This looks bad, I thought. It was one thing to throw eggs at a building, another to throw them at a bunch of people cowering behind shields. Why didn't their superiors bring them inside? Where had Joshua gone? I had a feeling that things were on the brink of getting out of control.

By this point, a whole pallet had arrived, stacked high with grey cartons of eggs, hundreds and hundreds of them. I've got to doing something, I thought, and hopped down from the flyover where I, like everyone else, had been watching the show unfold.

I went up to the place where several layers of cartons had been taken from the pallet and put on the ground. It was the supply point most of the egg throwers were drawing from. I could see back behind the front lines a very large pallet a metre or so tall that had hardly been touched – where were all these eggs coming from?

I put my foot lightly over the eggs and told people to stop. "It looks bad," I said. "There are all these foreign journalists about, and this is the image they're transmitting to the world: protesters raining eggs down on a few sorry cops who aren't fighting back. It just looks bad." I deliberately went with the effect argument ("it looks bad") rather than the moral argument ("it's wrong"). I didn't think the latter would be very persuasive just then.

I heard a voice behind me say, "Step away from the eggs. They don't belong to you. You have no business here."

I knew that voice. I turned around. "Francis! Fancy meeting you here!"

He smiled in recognition, then said in an affectionate but stern voice, "Move away from those eggs, Ah Tsung [as he called me], or you and I are going to have a problem."

I smiled back at him and stepped away. I didn't want any trouble with Francis. I didn't want any trouble with anyone. I'd made my point. The eggs continued to fly. The police continued to do nothing. Eventually, those officers getting pelted were brought into the station.

Later, Francis asked me, "What did you think you were doing?"

"I just didn't think it was cool to pelt a bunch of poor cops who weren't even fighting back with eggs. What's the point? It looks like bullying. It was almost as if their superiors kept them out there to make us look bad."

"C'mon, it's just eggs."

"Yeah, I guess I'm just a little concerned that when everything's so leaderless, it's often those who take the initiative who drive things, and we've got to be a little careful we aren't led in a direction that maybe isn't the best to go."

"Ya gotta go with the flow, brother."

"Not if the flow's going the wrong way. We've got the moral high ground. We should keep it. I don't care that much when it's just people attacking buildings – it's just a building, after all. But I get a little worried when I see people attacking people, even if they're cops. I saw a bunch of people stopping a guy who they thought was taking close-ups of protesters. They wanted him to open his phone and delete the pictures. He was reluctant. They started shoving him around a bit. I told them it's cool they want him to delete the photos, but they shouldn't beat him up. They assured me they wouldn't. Things calmed down a bit and I went on my way. That's the sort of situation I'm concerned about."

"Things are going to get worse before they're going to get better. You can't stop it. You just have to be ready for it."

"What does that mean?"

"It means what it means."

❋

Ten days later, on 1 July, another huge march. Well, OK, "only" half a million this time. It was the twenty-second anniversary of the handover of Hong Kong from the UK to the Chinese government, delivered like a present from one colonial power to the other, the Hong Kong people having no say in the matter. But for the CCP, it was an occasion to celebrate. In fact, the city's "return to the motherland" was the CCP's birthday present to itself, 1 July also being the anniversary of the founding of the Party.

For Hong Kong people, this year especially there was nothing to celebrate, and we wanted the regime to know it. There was a pro-democracy march every 1 July, which always stole the regime's thunder. Some years, it was huge. For example, in the year the Umbrella Movement broke out, 2014, it was half a million. But even in the off years, a hundred thousand would typically turn out. This was a half-a-million year. Organised by Civil Human Rights Front just like the marches of 9 and 16 June, it was peaceful.

Meanwhile, in front of Legco, a slow-motion break-in was taking place. Some of the young braves had got it into their heads that the thing to do was to ram metal poles into the exterior of Legco, lined with huge glass panes.

Now, this looks like a really bad idea, was my initial reaction. But by then, I'd learned not to say much: what did I know?

The poles didn't have much effect. The kids scavenged and came up with metal carts and all kinds of other jury-rigged contraptions that they rammed repeatedly into the plate glass, which ever so slowly began to crack and crack.

Police were nowhere to be seen outside the building, but they were right on the other side of the glass. You could watch them watching the protesters trying to break in. It took hours. It was like watching a car wreck about to occur in excruciatingly slow motion: you wanted to avert your eyes but kept peeking through your fingers.

Finally, towards evening, the breakthrough. I was outside the building watching it occur while also keeping my eye on a livestream from inside the building where police had pulled down the metal security shutters, rendering them invisible from the outside. They were gearing up.

The protesters broke through the glass panes, crossed the threshold and began trying to pry up the metal shutters. Just as they were about to succeed, sure to provoke a major confrontation, the strangest of things happened: the police disappeared. It really was almost like magic: one moment they were there, about to seriously pound some heads, the next they were gone.

The mystery of why the police disappeared has never been solved. Why would a police force simply step aside and allow protesters to storm the parliament? It makes no sense. The police gave some mealy-mouthed explanation about how they feared major injuries as a result of confrontations, but there were so many other ways they might have defended Legco but didn't – for example, by intervening beforehand from the outside and dispersing people long before they'd broken through.

At any rate, it was no more mister nice guy after that,

no more passive policing. The very next day, the police thundered that they would track down the culprits and round them up. And from then on, police violence was stepped up and continues to be the most prominent feature of the policing of the protests to this day. No more sit back and see what happens; attack before protesters have a chance to do anything; use overwhelming force to strike fear, panic and terror.

With the police gone, protesters flooded into the building, spray-painting the walls with graffiti, tearing down the portraits of former presidents (all regime lackeys) of the rigged body and breaking into the Legco chamber, the inner sanctum, where they blacked out the last bit of the emblem of the Hong Kong Special Administrative Region of the People's Republic of China.

And what was my reaction, I who had been ambivalent about the action from the start? Elation. For the first time ever in Hong Kong's post-handover history, the people were in the corridors of power. Of course I knew that actually Legco was pretty much powerless, at any rate not where the real power lay. Of course I knew both the action and the feeling were transitory. Of course, I knew that the police would arrive before long and there could be some very serious consequences for the break-in. But I couldn't help myself: it felt great, it felt cathartic. It was like a dream fulfilled, if ever so fleetingly.

After the Legco break-in, the foreign media erred again. Just as they assumed that Carrie Lam "suspending" the extradition bill would be enough to placate most protesters, they assumed that the Legco break-in would make most non-violent protesters and other Hong Kong people turn against the movement. Nothing could have been further from the truth.

And why didn't we? Because most people saw that non-violence had been strictly observed and practised for years, to almost no positive effect. So was it any surprise that young people in particular were willing to employ other methods? And really, what was so bad about targeting government property? We weren't attacking people. In fact, we were appalled that the CCP and the Hong Kong government were more concerned about damage to objects, such as PRC emblems and flags, than to people. No authorities expressed the least concern about the many people injured, some seriously, in the police attack of 12 June, but they raged over the Legco break-in.

It was especially after this event that one of the most important aspects of the movement fully emerged: the strong solidarity, unity and trust among all protesters, regardless of our age differences, our political differences, our differences in terms of strategy and tactics. Alongside this was our commitment to leaderlessness, to no one taking over the "main stage", as the saying went. Precepts arose such as not cutting ties with anyone and always supporting one another. We recognised and respected one another. It was a feeling that ran very deep, and it was what made the movement strong and carried us through difficult times.

It wasn't just theoretical or philosophical; it was born of personal relationships, like mine with Francis, and because of that, in spite of whatever disagreements we might have, there was a deep trust, perhaps even a kind of love. This trust, this love, went out to everyone we'd met and fought beside in the many months of struggle. How else could it be that over all those months I'd never once so much as got in an argument or had a falling-out or even really got angry with a single "comrade", to use Francis's term, that never once during all those months was there a public disagreement among protesters. This unity, this love, was one of the things that made being part of the freedom struggle so deeply gratifying: we were all in it together, fighting alongside one another, for the same thing.

It also made us hard to crush. And it made the movement effective, the combination of entirely non-violent protests and more aggressive, disruptive protests. It kept the government and the police off balance, on the back foot. It kept them guessing. They never knew what was coming. Non-violent protests had become too easy for them to contain and ignore: Oh, a million marched? So what. Oh, two million marched? So what again. But breaking into Legco – now that provoked a reaction! And didn't hurt a soul, by the way.

✻

After the Legco break-in, as the protests went on, Francis and I rarely saw each other, and we had a tacit mutual pact never to inquire about the other's exploits. It was simply the way it was with protesters: you trusted one another, and the less you knew, the better. I didn't know if Francis had been at Legco that night or not. I didn't see him, but then again, everyone was masked. I might have run into him on numerous occasions after that without even recognising him.

But we developed an ongoing Telegram discussion. We checked in with each other regularly to make sure we were safe and to debate the latest events. I always wanted to know what he thought about what had just happened.

I was always trying to assess opinion among protesters. The way I did it was to ask people I thought pretty much represented certain positions, the moderates, the radicals, the young braves, the peaceful, rational types, old people, young people, middle-aged people. It was a method that never failed.

Plus, I knew whatever I got from Francis, it would be real. When you've been fanatically dedicated to a cause for a long time, you recognise other fanatics. Francis and I were fellow fanatics.

We agreed almost entirely on politics. What we frequently disagreed on was how the movement should be conducted, on tactics. But we always cursed and insulted one another in the best of spirits. I told him when he said something stupid; he said the same to me.

I admired his dedication, his vehemence, his passion, his zealotry. Didn't every struggle that faced great odds need this kind of "warrior spirit", as Francis himself called it? Didn't it need people willing to die for the cause?

That willingness to die was not just bravado. Borrowed from the US revolutionaries and spray-painted on the walls of the city, "Give me liberty or give me death" was more than just a slogan. Few seemed to understand that the kids really meant it. That didn't mean they would recklessly throw their lives away. In fact, one of the tenets of the movement was to protect yourself and others, not to take any unnecessary risks, always to seek to live to fight another day. What it did mean was that many believed the day would come when a decision had to be made about whether to lay your life on the line, and it was best to prepare mentally for it in advance, so that you would know what to do when that day arrived.

I took some of Francis's more extreme pronouncements as expressions of that passion, ascribing them to his natural garrulousness, his bluster. Sometimes I'd say to him, "I doubt you really believe that yourself", as when he broached the idea of getting arms from members of the Ukrainian far-right Azov Battalion who passed through Hong Kong as supposed protest tourists.

"But they're fascists," I said. "They're anti-Semites. They beat up Gypsies."

"Gypsies and Jews are no concern of ours," he said.

To which I said, "I doubt you really believe that yourself. Of course Gypsies and Jews are our business, just like Uighurs and all oppressed peoples of the world are. We stand in solidarity with all of them and hope they stand in solidarity with us. If we want a different Hong Kong, we must build it on solid values, and allying with fascists is definitely not the right way to do that; it's how you corrupt a movement."

Invoking the Uighurs always got him. He had a soft spot in his heart for them. He had a vision that one day, the Uighurs, Tibetans, Hongkongers and Taiwanese would rise up and launch a multi-front attack on the Communists. This would then inspire the Chinese to throw off their shackles and rise up against their oppressors, embroiling the Communists in a civil war they could not win.

I hope so, I said, because otherwise the Communists and their Chinese supporters will annihilate us.

Sometimes I wondered if I had too much faith in his basically good heart, his decency, his honour; I wondered if I deliberately overlooked what I didn't want to hear by translating it from the literal into no more than an expression of his passion for the cause, his love for his city, his feelings of anger, his desire for vengeance. A journalist I once sent his way – he was a sound-bite gold mine – said, "He loves to bluster but he's really a pussycat." My opinion on that went back and forth, but basically, my faith in him didn't waver.

Francis's talk of arms and getting the most retrograde of armed groups in the world to supply the freedom struggle wasn't all just bluster. He really believed it had got to the point where only armed uprising could push it further. It was our only chance: provoke a People's Liberation Army occupation and then fight a nasty guerrilla war. And it wasn't just him. I'd been hearing this kind of talk for years since the Umbrella Movement, but it had increased since the protests began. Almost always from young people – young men, to be precise. Maybe not ISIS or Azov Battalion – Francis's outrageous examples were indeed one of a kind – but the idea of escalation to something beyond what we had done up to now was definitely in the air.

As preposterous as an armed uprising in Hong Kong might sound, was it really any more unrealistic than any other scenario under CCP rule? That was the nature of the regime: it gave Hongkongers no solution of any kind, no way out; it turned every Hong Kong person who looked at the situation honestly into a closet separatist. And the Party propaganda line that separatists were stirring up trouble in Hong Kong thereby became a self-fulfilling prophecy: not because Hong Kong people were fervently in favour of independence (about one in six were) but because they could see no other way out. The pundits said independence was absurdly unrealistic. But was it any more so than genuine universal suffrage? Who really believed the Party would ever give us that? Just about everyone across the board, both in Hong Kong and abroad, supported it even as they had no idea how to bring it about.

And anyway, not too long ago, the idea that young protesters would be fighting running battles in the streets with police over months would have seemed almost as absurd as a fully armed uprising.

That was, as Francis saw it, the direction things were going, and we might as well recognise it, admit it to ourselves, embrace and prepare for it. To him, people like me just refused to accept reality. We were in denial. Wake up. You want your freedom? You have to be willing to fight for it. To the death. If not, then you don't really value your freedom all that much, do you? Maybe you don't even deserve it.

Meanwhile, as the crackdown became more severe, the actions of some protesters escalated. Throughout, the vast majority remained non-violent, but frontliners employed increasingly aggressive methods: barricading roads; disrupting transport; vandalising traffic lights, MTR stations, Chinese state-owned enterprises (especially banks), pro-Communist shops and businesses; throwing bricks and petrol bombs at police; and even occasionally attacking civilians, the only practice I unequivocally condemned, even as I understood that these were excesses committed by a tiny minority, not a common, agreed or approved tactic. Still, they were our excesses, for which we were all responsible and which we had to try to prevent.

How did I, an inveterate proponent of non-violence, square it all? Did I let my standards slip? Did I betray my principles? Had I become an opportunist? To the world, I defended all protesters. I was provoked by the patronising tone of know-it-all Westerners who said things like "I support all peaceful protests in HK" from the security of their rights-respecting democracies. With fellow protesters, especially frontliners like Francis, I argued. Our mutual trust could withstand the fiercest disagreements.

To the world I said, Look at your double standards regarding violence. Some political revolutionary violence was acceptable, even valorised; other violence was condemned. You want your Hong Kong protesters nice and cuddly, so you can feel all warm inside supporting pet freedom fighters. Once you enter into the logic of violence, once you allow that some violence is acceptable or justifiable – and if you believe police and armies, the state monopolisation of violence, legitimate, then you have entered into this logic – then you at least had to consider seriously the idea that fighting against oppressive state violence with force could be at least equally justifiable, especially in cases where the state violence was tyrannical and not underpinned by the legitimacy conferred by democracy.

Once you allow that armed rebellion against dictatorship may be justifiable, then the question becomes, What terms of engagement are justifiable? In this respect, it had to be said that the terms of engagement set by frontliners, who, remember, had no leader, were quite strict and generally adhered to with a high degree of discipline. For instance, remarkably, there was no looting whatsoever. Attacks on government buildings and pro-Communist shops and businesses such as the MTR – the city's subway system, 70 per cent owned by the government – were acceptable, though some found the attacks on shops and the MTR debatable and preferred boycotts. Using bricks and petrol bombs to defend oneself against police was acceptable, especially considering the level of force used by police against protesters (more than 30,000 missiles shot at us in six months: tear gas rounds, rubber bullets, sponge grenades, beanbag rounds, not to mention the batons and pepper spray). Attacking other citizens, especially unarmed civilians, was unacceptable except in self-defence (as when attacked by thugs).

After reviewing the terms of engagement, it seemed to me that those who denounced violence were doing so either from a position of complete pacifism (and when you scratched beneath the surface, there were few genuine, consistent pacifists in the world) or from the position that even the undemocratic and tyrannical state is legitimate, therefore its monopoly on use of violence (against citizens, it must be emphasised) was legitimate, and therefore use of violence against the state was illegitimate.

In other words, these weren't just kids irresponsibly playing at being revolutionaries. There was a clear rationale and logic to their actions. If you disagreed with them, the least you should do is articulate your own clear rationale and logic for doing so.

Yes, this proponent of non-violence had come a long way from objecting to pelting a few cops with eggs. At least in my thinking. I would still object to it, and say so; I just wouldn't try to stop it. I hadn't engaged in any of the so-called violent actions myself. Even if I fully approved of and believed in them, I doubt I would have been able to bring myself to commit them: I would have been hopeless at that kind of thing. (Francis's answer: "Anyone can learn to throw a Molotov cocktail, even you; I didn't know myself when this all started.")

When in November I came across Yangyang Cheng's essay on trying to have a discussion with her mother about Hong Kong, I thought, She took the words right out of my mouth. How could a scientist originally from the PRC but now living in the US be able to articulate this better than I, who was living it? Like me, she didn't outright condone or support the aggressive, destructive, disruptive actions of protesters but suggested that people needed to think more carefully about the issue and contextualise it.

"In a society that values decorum more than justice, condemning violence is an easy way to feel good about oneself without asking the hard questions: Who is violent? Where is the violence directed at? What places do the respective parties occupy in structures of power?"

She continued, "Power incentivises forgiving and forgetting. Law and order are often code names for the normalisation of systematic violence, demanding that the oppressed accept structural injustices as the default condition of life... It is much easier to train the eye on a burning campus than on the structures of power behind the flame. It is much more comforting for the docile to condemn violence than to confront the cost of liberation."

I also appreciated her tribute to Hong Kong: "I see in the people of Hong Kong a version of China that is still possible: a rejection of the false binary between prosperity and freedom, an assertion of national identity independent from the state, a breakup with the imperial fantasy, an imagination of justice and the willingness to demand it." But I wondered if that was still possible in China.

While, before the world, I defended all protesters, within the movement, I constantly debated with Francis and others about the efficacy and morality of violence, the terms of engagement, how the rest of the world perceived us.

"I can tolerate a lot of what the regime and the media are calling violence, but protesters have to stop beating pro-CCP people. That's terrible."

"Pourquoi? We wouldn't have had acted that way if we hadn't been assaulted first. Or if we knew police would protect us. But police are on the side of the thugs attacking us."

"No, we have to be honest: on several occasions, protesters have beaten people who were not attacking them. It's deplorable and it must stop. Yesterday, I saw them do it to a guy in Sha Tin, on Friday to a guy in Central. It's bullying; it's the worst behaviour; it's not valiant or brave. It upsets me very much to see people on my side acting like that."

"I still say they deserve it if they provoked our comrades, even if only verbally. It's not very clever to express dissent among an angry, volatile crowd. And I'm pretty sure our comrades won't assault random passers-by like those thugs do."

"No, if we do that, we're as low as the Communist thugs. Attacking CCP property is OK, fighting back against police is OK, fighting back against thugs is OK, but leave ordinary people alone."

"Those 'victims' must have had done something to get their asses whipped."

"They said something, so what? We all have the right to speak."

"Honestly, I can't really help much if some blue-ribbon retards try to pick a fight with a crowd of comrades."

"If it ever happens where I am, I'll protect the blue-ribbon retards."

"Don't: you'll risk the wrath of our comrades. You ever heard of Karl Popper? As paradoxical as it may seem, defending tolerance requires not tolerating the intolerant."

"We fight intolerance with words, not with fists. And for the most part, protesters have been amazingly disciplined, all the more reason to stop the excesses, which are exceptional, not the norm. In fighting monsters, we mustn't become monsters ourselves. That's what happened to the Communists. Resisting the Communists means not acting like them."

※

In mid-October, a police officer was slashed in the neck. It happened in Kwun Tong, in the exact place I had been only a half hour before. I'd left when I felt the police closing in. Not long after, they trapped protesters in a mall. Then they made to enter the mall, crossing a pedestrian bridge. A video of the incident began circulating on social media not long after it occurred: a large group of police officers in full riot gear walk past. Suddenly, out of the corner of the screen, a hand appears and slashes an officer across the neck with what looks like a boxcutter. It happens so quickly, you have to rewind and view it several times before you feel you've seen it. The police immediately apprehend the nearest young person. The officer who was attacked is among those who wrestle him to the ground, a sign that the injury was perhaps not so grave as it initially appeared. It is rumoured that they got the wrong guy; the real culprit slipped away.

This came just days after a notorious incident: a teenager had been shot in the chest, point-blank, by a police officer who later claimed he'd done it in self-defence – the lives of himself and his fellow officers were in danger. The kid was still in serious condition but it looked like he would miraculously pull through. The neck-slashing attack on the cop had about it a whiff of revenge.

It could not possibly be construed as defensive. Much of what was characterised as protester violence against police was defensive in nature. For example, petrol bombs were thrown at police shooting tear gas, rubber bullets, sponge grenades and beanbag rounds in order to keep a certain distance between police and protesters, usually as police attacked and protesters retreated. But this slashing appeared entirely gratuitous: what purpose could it serve apart from injuring the officer? It could only be justified in terms of war: enemy combatants are fair game, regardless of the situation.

I asked Francis his opinion: "Do you think it was OK to slash the policeman's neck in Kwun Tong?"

"Fully support it. But slash is an exaggeration. It was just a shallow nick. ACAB." Francis was an aficionado of English and loved to sprinkle his speech with fancy acronyms, sayings, phrases. At first, I'd had no idea what ACAB meant. But he said it so often, almost like a personal motto, that I got used to it: All Cops Are Bastards. "Any cops with a conscience would have quit by now. Many did. Those who stayed – no matter if they're directly responsible for abuses or not – are considered the evil of banality." Sometimes his fancy English phrases were a bit off.

"It's the banality of evil."

"Thanks. I always get that wrong."

"The attack was not in self-defence. It was gratuitous. It was intended solely to injure. That man has a family too."

"He murdered others with families. And he fucking got away with the atrocity with the blood debt on his hands. That's why we're gonna kill EVERY SINGLE ONE OF THEM, ALL 30,000. If we don't exterminate the Communists, it'll be impossible to establish a free society since communism itself is an ideology of intolerance. Sounds contradictory because we have to carry out extermination to achieve freedom. But I guess that's how the world works. I guess the best way is to exterminate once and for all and then never carry out such acts again."

"Once you start killing to get power, you must continue killing to keep it. You become a hostage to your own violence. In short, you become a Communist, everything you detest."

"Why? From my POV it's possible to stop killing with killing. My view is, if you can empower people by founding a liberal democracy after you've done the killing, you can get out of the vicious cycle of violence started by the Commies."

We don't talk for some hours. As I go about my day, I begin to wonder whether I'd seen him there that day. It was hard to know; everyone was so well masked. But the more I thought about it, I could have sworn I recognised him spray-painting "liberate Hong Kong, revolution of our times" on the shiny floor of the mall. It was his husky frame that gave him away; most young Hong Kong men were on the scrawny side. Even at the time, the thought briefly flashed through my mind, but it was hardly the sort of impression I paid any attention to in the heat of the moment.

Later in the day, I texted him on Telegram: *Was it you?* A half hour later, these words appeared on my screen: *You know the answer to that.*

✻

After that, I didn't talk to him again for some time. Not because I held anything against him or had any particular suspicion or knew the answer to my question, but because things got busy. The events of the protests were continually overtaking me; I felt as if always trying to catch up.

Then we heard Nancy was not doing well, Nancy who'd introduced us, Nancy with whom Francis had been arrested during the Battle of Lung Wo Road in what now seemed like a bygone era, Nancy who'd been diagnosed with cancer while fighting her conviction for obstructing police.

One day Francis and I meet by coincidence at a protest on Nathan Road, the main thoroughfare of Kowloon, which had seen many protests, many fierce battles.

During a lull, he says, "Hey, we have to go visit Nancy."

"Yes, I've been meaning to."

"Let's go now. The hospital's nearby."

"Dressed like that?" I laugh, gesturing to his full gear.

"Yeah, sure. Why not? Once we get out of here, I'll take it off and go disguised as a normal human being."

On the way there, I turn to him and say, out of the blue, apropos of nothing, "You motherfucker. If they catch you, they're going to charge you with attempted murder."

"Don't worry; they won't catch me."

"Watch yourself."

"Don't worry; I will." He doesn't want to fight with me. He sounds a little sheepish.

It isn't that often I can tell him off and he actually listens to me. It strikes me: at this moment, this is a little kid in a big kid's body. He wants to be told off, he wants someone to tell him, Watch yourself. This is a young man with the weight of the world on his shoulders.

Every young brave sets out at the start of the day in full awareness that if he or she gets caught, he or she could end up serving up to 10 years in prison – the maximum penalty for riot, the charge that's been slapped on over half of the protesters who've been brought to court. "This could be the start of 10 years in prison," he says to himself as he heads out. He also feels it's up to him to liberate Hong Kong. No one wants to fuck up, to dishonour the struggle. Whenever someone does, the first reaction is always: it must be a police plant; it must be a Communist infiltrator. No one can ever quite bring themselves to believe it just might be one of our own.

When we arrive, she's in bed. The nurse tells us she's just had a session of chemotherapy. She looks terrible, disoriented. At first, I'm not even sure she recognises us.

We don't talk much. A few awkward pleasantries that sound all the more inane against the background silence of the situation.

Francis and I feel embarrassed, about the fact that we're healthy, about the fact we're going about our business of liberating Hong Kong in the world out there while she's stuck in here, about the fact that life goes on while she's dying.

We wonder if we should tell her about the protests, but she doesn't seem to be interested in anything. She looks like she's merely enduring our visit. It's taking all of her effort to be polite, to appear present, to interact with us.

As we are about to leave, in a weak voice, almost a whisper, looking directly into our eyes, she says the only thing during our visit that sounds like she really means it, the only words meant just for us: "Whatever else may happen, keep fighting, boys. For me."

"We will," we say, "we will." On our way out, we don't have much to say. We're going back to the protest. I can feel an adrenalin surge going through Francis. He says he has to nip off and run an errand. I know whatever he has to do, he doesn't want me along.

We stand silent for a moment at the hospital entrance before parting ways.

"Being sick sucks," says Francis.

"Yeah," I say. "And being fatally ill sucks even more."

"Yeah," he says. "It sucks more than most things."

"Yeah," I say. "It sucks more than almost anything else."

"More than being arrested."

"Or tear-gassed."

"Or pepper-sprayed."

"Or beaten up."

"Or shot."

"Or even losing an eye."

"Yes, much more."

"And much more than dying in the struggle. At least then people will remember you for that."

"Or not."

"Or not."

I suddenly want to cry.

I've become inured to so much suffering over the months, so much pain. The exceptional becomes the norm. And then, when you least expect it, the dam breaks. I have to say something to keep from sobbing. All I can choke out is:

"We've come a long way, Francis."

"Yes, and we still have a long way to go, Ah Tsung."

"Let's get started."

"Again."

"Again and again."

"Let's do it for Nancy."

"And for all the ones who can no longer be with us."

"For all the ones who are going down before freedom is won."

"For all of our brothers and sisters in the struggle."

"For all oppressed people everywhere."

He reaches down and gives me an awkward hug.

"Stay safe, brother."

"You too."

SANCTUARY

兄弟爬山 各自努力

We all climb the mountain together,
each contributing in their own way

– protest maxim

Of the many police attacks I'd experienced in nearly four months of protests, the one in Wan Chai on 1 October was certainly among the most intense.

The situation was initially almost a replay of similar scenes that had unfolded along that stretch of Hong Kong Island: when the police wished to clear protesters from near government headquarters in Admiralty, they would push them to Queensway, a block to the south, and, from there, down Queensway eastward past police headquarters.

They achieved this push primarily with tear gas barrages, often accompanied by the so-called raptors, the Special Tactical Squad, rushing out from police lines to randomly snatch and grab protesters for arrest.

They would then slowly, deliberately and predictably continue to push us down Hennessy Road towards Causeway Bay, in the hope that most of us would eventually disperse.

But after this had become almost a routine, they decided an insufficient number were dispersing, and they began situating large numbers of riot police in Causeway Bay, thus sandwiching protesters between those police and the police pushing us in that direction.

This led to volatile situations and brutal encounters. Protesters were beaten before, during and after arrest. Undercover police officers disguised as protesters fired live warning shots into the air when they were discovered and surrounded by protesters. It had got to the point where the feeling hung in the air that it would take so little for something to go terribly wrong. Not only that, but protesters quickly adapted and were able to avoid the police dragnet.

So on 1 October, the police did something new: after pushing protesters eastward past police headquarters, as in the past, they conducted a blitzkrieg attack, very rapidly charging from two different directions at protesters while launching massive tear gas barrages.

I happened to be on Queen's Road East at that point. Police were charging us from the west, shooting tear gas. As we moved eastward, other protesters ran out of side streets from the north, pursued by police raining tear gas down on them.

Then, up ahead, another line of riot police appeared. We were surrounded on three sides. On the fourth, to the south, there was only the mountain. We were trapped and being hit with tear gas from two directions.

Ever since 12 June, when police trapped protesters at Citic Tower across from the Legco building, leaving them nowhere to disperse, and attacked them with tear gas, human rights organisations and crowd control experts had said tear gas is intended to make people disperse and it shouldn't be used in situations in which people have nowhere to go. And yet there were police doing exactly that again on 1 October. The tear gas was so thick, it felt like a chemical weapon attack.

In the nearly four months of protests, I'd eaten a lot of tear gas and had become quite adept at judging just how much I could tolerate. But on 1 October, not only were the barrages more intense, there was also nowhere to run to get away from them.

My eyes watered and felt as if they were swelling shut. Peering through slits and tears, I could hardly see. On my skin was the sensation of burning, not so different from when hit by pepper spray, another "non-lethal" weapon I'd become very familiar with. As I ran, my chest began to tighten and seize up. This must be what it's like to have a heart attack, I thought. I was coughing uncontrollably and spitting repeatedly to keep the gas from getting deep into my lungs.

Hundreds of protesters were bunched up at the bottom of a narrow staircase leading up towards the mountain. They were trying to squeeze up it. It looked like the sort of situation in which a stampede could occur. There was no way I was going to get up there before the police descended on us.

I turned around, fighting through the thick crowd of protesters, and ran in the opposite direction back towards the police. It was one of those counter-intuitive intuitions. Or the impulse of a quasi-claustrophobe: I'd rather face that risk than risk being trapped in a stampede.

I managed to find a small gap in police lines that led to a cop-less side street. This was no escape, though: I knew there were more police on the street up ahead, as they had initially come from that direction. I'd emerged from the worst of the crush but was still trapped.

✻

Most shops and restaurants in the area, as throughout the city, were closed that day. When I had first ventured out in the morning, never had I seen the city so quiet. A cold, deathly silence. The city was bracing itself. Often during the protests, life could go on as normal just a few streets away. It was almost surreal. Sometimes when police shot tear gas at protesters, they couldn't avoid hitting traffic, passers-by. It took a lot for Hong Kong people to put life on hold. Today was such a day.

The Party was celebrating 70 years of dictatorship; we called it a "day of mourning". Protests had been called across the city. What did it say about a country, I wondered to myself as I walked to the march that morning, trying to avoid police roadblocks along the way, when on the day designated by its rulers as a celebration of the nation, the seventieth anniversary of the founding of the republic, a part of the territory they controlled was in open rebellion?

As the biggest military parade ever was being held in Beijing – which simply fuelled our perception of the regime as essentially fascist in nature, equating military strength with greatness – across Hong Kong, the people rose up, in

Tuen Mun, Sha Tin, Tsuen Wan, Wong Tai Sin, Sham Shui Po, Yau Tsim Mong, North Point, Wan Chai, Causeway Bay, Central and Sheung Wan.

A march had been planned. Like all other marches for nearly a month, it was banned by the police. Hundreds of thousands turned up anyway. We went from Causeway Bay to Central, the original terminus. Many kept going towards the Liaison Office, headquarters of the PRC government's official contact with the city, a logical end point on a day the regime called national day.

On 28 July, police had been so intent on guarding Hong Kong government headquarters that they'd let their guard down: protesters had been able to get close enough to the Liaison Office that they defaced the PRC emblem on its façade with black paint bombs. The regime raged, reinforcing a general perception in the city that it cared much more about state symbols than people: this was an attack on its sovereignty! (As if the people weren't the true sovereigns.)

It had nothing to say about the fact that that same night, more than a hundred white-shirted thugs associated with the regime attacked citizens in Yuen Long, up near the border with the PRC. They beat people with metal poles and rattan sticks. At the end of it all, at least 45 people were hospitalised. Police didn't respond to repeated emergency calls, and there was no police presence at the scene until more than a half hour after the alarm was sounded. By that point, most of the thugs had melted away, although police were seen cordially conversing with several who were still holding their weapons, as if they were allies.

For many Hong Kong people, the contrast between the Party and Hong Kong government's reactions to the state symbol's defacement and the thug attack, between the police responses to the two incidents, was a moment of reckoning, a turning point from which there was no going back.

Since then, the Liaison Office had become one of the city's main fortresses, along with government headquarters, police headquarters, police stations and a few other complexes such as the express rail terminus. The government and police essentially existed on fortressed islands dotting the city, surrounded by a hostile populace. The government never ventured forth. The police did so only to attack protesters.

Despite being banned, the 1 October march was allowed to proceed largely unhindered down the main thoroughfares of Hong Kong Island. This was a sharp contrast to two days before, when police attacked the start of the Global Anti-Totalitarianism Day march with tear gas. In vain: there were so many people in the side streets all around the march starting point that police simply couldn't attack us all. Once the tear gas attack passed, they spilled out into Hennessy Road, and the march defiantly proceeded. On that day, Hong Kong solidarity protests had been held in dozens of cities around the world; only in Hong Kong was the protest attacked, the contrast bringing into stark relief how rapidly the right to freedom of assembly in the city was being eroded.

But on the 1st, after banning the march, the police backed off, initially at least. There were so many other protests in other parts of the city that the police couldn't afford to concentrate all their force on us. In fact, as was their wont, police were the most brutal in the districts, and especially in the poorest parts of town. That's also where the protesters were the toughest; they didn't give up or back down, even in the face of overwhelming force.

*

While shops were shuttered throughout the city, in that small side street where I found myself, restaurants had opened to shelter protesters fleeing the police. So many people were crammed in, the small restaurants looked like crowded subway cars. They had no more room and were pulling down their shutters again before the police came.

And then what seemed almost magical happened: the doors of apartment buildings opened. Residents shouted out into the street, urging fleeing protesters to enter.

Just before I got to the end of the street, I ducked into an open doorway. The man holding the door said, "Keep going up until you reach the top." It was a decrepit old walk-up. On my way up, I passed three apartments with their doors open. Dozens of protesters were inside each flat. When I got to the roof, dozens more were there, sitting cross-legged, pressed up against one another.

Stepping over people, I crept to the roof's edge. Down below, the street itself was deserted, but at both ends I could see dozens of riot police. They were looking around in astonishment, as if asking themselves, "Where did they all go?" Indeed, we'd disappeared into thin air thanks to the residents of that street. Between the restaurants and the apartment buildings, there must have been several hundred of us hidden there.

Up on the roof, there wasn't much talking. People seemed tired or stunned or wary. I tried to strike up conversations without success. Then the mood became clear: a guy next to me said a young man had been shot in Tsuen Wan.

A man near the door motioned for me to come over. "Do you want to see the footage?" he asked.

I really didn't but said OK. He showed me a video of the young man lying on the ground bleeding.

"Here's another of him getting shot," someone else offered: a police officer shot him at point-blank range, aiming at his upper body.

"That must be fatal," I said.

No one said anything. What do you say about something like that?

"How is he?" I asked.

No one knew; he'd been taken to a hospital. Strange, I thought, that we, hiding from police in one part of the city, could so readily view someone getting shot by police in another part of the city so soon after it happened.

"Compared to being shot," I said, "tear gas isn't much." It was only when he stood up that I noticed the man near the door who showed me the initial video was a dwarf. I hadn't known if he was a protester or not, but when I saw how short his legs were, I assumed he lived in the building and was one of those providing refuge. He had a beard, a worldly face, like an explorer who had sailed the seven seas.

I peered over the edge again. Past the end of the street, there was a block-wide playground, on the other side of which I could see one of the police water cannon trucks and a Unimog, an armoured vehicle, in the road, their red and blue lights flashing. They stayed there motionless for upwards of a half hour, waiting for the officers on foot to finish their mop-up operations.

A police helicopter could be heard in the distance. Before long it was hovering overhead, though so far above, we couldn't be sure how clearly it might be able to see us. Taking no chances, we crammed into the building's stairwell.

After about an hour, it became clear that most police had moved eastward towards Causeway Bay, where we heard there were still protesters on the street. Most of us decided to leave. I said thank you to all of the residents I could find on the way down the stairs. They just shrugged and smiled.

The man who let me in was still at the bottom of the stairs near the door, standing sentry. He had crutches and moved with difficulty. He gave me the biggest smile of them all and in that moment appeared the kindest of men, saintly; it was easy to imagine him in monk's robes.

As soon as we emerged onto the street, people came up to us and told us which streets to take to avoid police. They had scouted the neighbourhood, and their intelligence was accurate: I didn't meet a single cop as I made my way out of Wan Chai. I was thirsty, and since all shops were closed, I stopped at a church open to protesters and got some water.

✳

The English word "sanctuary" derives from the Latin "sanctus", holy. The early use of the word "sanctuarium" referred to a church or other sacred place where, by the law of the medieval church, a fugitive was immune from arrest.

This act of giving sanctuary, in all its various forms, was not only moving but also one of the most profound and perhaps even spiritual acts of the protests. Even those not on the streets protesting were protesting. Everyone contributed to the resistance in his or her own way. 兄弟爬山 各自努力 was one of the slogans of the movement: "We all climb the mountain together, each contributing in their own way." The majority of the population was united against the regime. The story of that Wan Chai street was not exceptional. It was a moment in time, gone in a flash, but the kindness of strangers I'd experience repeatedly.

Just days before, on 29 September, Global Anti-

Totalitarianism Day, I'd been retreating together with about 2,000 protesters towards Causeway Bay. We got word of many riot police there and decided to head southward, but every street we came to, we saw police at the end of it. Eventually, we had no choice but to go into Happy Valley, a prosperous neighbourhood that had seen little of the protests. It was *terra incognita* for most of us. Once there, we felt safer, but we knew it was just a matter of time before the police would flush us out, and we didn't know where to go.

Security guards emerged from luxury high-rises and offered directions. A taxi driver had seen us and alerted his colleagues. Before long, dozens of taxis started to arrive. Having heard of our situation on Telegram, private drivers pulled up, rolled down their windows and announced their destinations. Protesters hopped in. Within about a half hour, of those 2,000 protesters, no one but myself and a few others remained on the street.

Among protesters, a cardinal rule was, you never leave anyone behind. Because I was older and less of a police target than the younger protesters, my role was often to remain until last to make sure everyone got out. With only a few of us left, I changed out of my black outfit and headed back across police lines. Along the way, residents who witnessed and helped the evacuation gave me knowing smiles and thumbs-up. "Stay safe, stay safe," they said.

Turning a corner, I almost ran right into dozens of riot cops. They looked me over suspiciously, but I was alone and pretended I was talking on the phone. I must have looked very absorbed in the conversation – they let me pass.

The solidarity of the population at large manifested itself in ways both symbolic and practical. Earlier on 1 October, the same day hundreds of us found refuge in the restaurants and apartment buildings of that side street in Wan Chai, we marched along Connaught Road, a major thoroughfare in Central, towards the Liaison Office, bringing traffic to a standstill. A long line of buses was stuck. One might imagine the passengers irate at their situation, but as we passed, they put their hands up against the windows, fingers spread wide, imitating the gesture made by protesters shouting, "Five demands, not one less". Protesters pressed their hands up against the bus windows so that they matched the bus passengers' hands, palm to palm, finger to finger. Such a simple, small act; it cost nothing, but it was a reaching out, across a gulf. Hong Kong people are not given to expressions of emotion in public, which made the connection felt through the buses' plate glass windows all the more powerful, as if those hands pressed together gave an electric charge. We refused to live just in our atomised cells, isolated from one another; we would not allow the regime to divide and conquer us. We are a people, I thought, a people.

This widespread solidarity got substantial media coverage perhaps for the first time on 1 September, during what was dubbed Hong Kong's Dunkirk. Protesters had gone to the airport to disrupt services, as they had done earlier in August. But now a court injunction had been obtained by the Airport Authority against protests there, and it was heavily guarded by police.

Protesters succeeded in causing disruptions, but when police began to crack down, protesters started to evacuate. The problem was, most public transport, including buses and the Airport Express train, had been shut down. What few buses were still running people feared the police would stop-and-search. And you couldn't walk out of there so easily: the airport lies on a sparsely populated island, Hong Kong's biggest, some 35 kilometres from the city centre.

Some protesters walked the five kilometres to Tung Chung, the nearest place where people actually lived, planning to take the MTR from there, but MTR had shut the station at the police's behest, and there were rumours that police would stop-and-search any buses or ferries out of Tung Chung. In fact, it wasn't long before the police arrived there as well. Some Tung Chung residents took protesters into their homes and hid them overnight.

Other protesters kept marching along the main highway on their way towards the city. It was then that the rescue operation swung into motion, coordinated primarily on Telegram groups. Hundreds of cars drove out to the highway and picked up protesters. Police were waiting at bus stops and ferry piers to catch protesters, but due to the citizen rescue operation, they managed to catch almost no one.

That was one of the most visible instances of citizen solidarity with protesters. But more pervasive, enduring and influential were quieter forms: the donation of supplies to protesters, monetary donations to all kinds of protest organisations set up to aid arrested and injured protesters and to publicise the cause abroad. People took young protesters into their homes when they got thrown out by parents who objected to their participation in the protests, this in spite of the fact that most Hong Kong people live in shoeboxes with little to no extra space. They let young protesters stash their gear with them. They helped hundreds of protesters who feared arrest and prosecution to escape to Taiwan. When protesters were arrested or injured, a whole network stepped forward to provide aid, including lawyers, social workers and the Hidden Clinic support network of doctors, physiotherapists and other medical professionals that provided free treatment to those who feared that going to public hospitals could lead to arrest. When protesters started getting fired from their jobs or having financial difficulties, when young people started being threatened with never being able to find a job in the city because of their involvement in the freedom struggle, an online shop was founded with the express purpose of providing jobs, a Telegram group hooked up hundreds of jobless protesters with sympathetic employers, a well-to-do "yellow" businessman ("yellow" businesses supported the protesters; "blue" supported the police) opened a vocational training programme that hooked young protesters up with jobs afterwards. The list goes on and on.

This was the story of the protests that couldn't be captured in dramatic images of police and protesters clashing on the city streets. Hong Kong people were continually resourceful, innovative, civic-minded. They set up support networks and infrastructure that amounted to a kind of parallel society. In doing so, they were creating the society we envisioned and strove for, the sort of place we hoped Hong Kong would one day become. It was all self-organising, a beautiful anarchy, a society freely constituted without authorities or a governing body.

The leaderlessness of the movement was frequently remarked on. Compared to movements with clearly recognisable leaders and decision-making structures and processes, there was much truth to that characterisation. But it also had the tendency to obscure the fact that there were so many leaders in so many different areas of the movement, everyone rushing to fill the gaps they felt needed to be filled with whatever expertise, experience or resources they felt capable of providing.

At the root of this solidarity, this resistance, was a feeling. We recognised something in each other, a common purpose, a common identity: we are Hong Kong people. We're united by the desire to defend our home. This unity couldn't be crushed by force. In fact, threats by the Party and police attacks reinforced it, drawing us closer together, showing how our only true, reliable resource was ourselves, our mutual support networks.

That afternoon, as I walked out of the neighbourhood where I'd been sheltered from the police, I felt miserable, and not for the first time: as many times as I walked away from a protest elated, I left dejected. For a moment, I'd forgotten that however much the police brutalised us and put us on the run, we'd managed to ruin the Party's national day party. Instead, I thought, We haven't won anything; we haven't accomplished anything; in fact, we've continually retreated and been chased into hiding. How many comrades have been arrested, beaten, how many have I left behind? I felt as if I'd betrayed them. I thought of the young man shot in the chest earlier in the day. I felt empty, defeated: what good can ever come of this? I thought of just how much more suffering the Party, the government, the police were capable of inflicting on us – it seemed limitless.

But then I slapped myself: I thought back over the course of events. I thought of the common feeling shared by protesters and most Hong Kong people. I thought of the people who had hidden us in their homes, the sacrifices people were willing to make, the risks they were willing to take, the suffering they were willing to endure, and I also felt heartened. This, I thought, forged through the common experience of adversity, is how a nation is born.

RUNNING WITH THE KIDS

香港人加油⋯香港人反抗⋯香港人報仇

Hong Kong people, add oil! … Hong Kong people, resist! … Hong Kong people, take revenge!

Throughout the protests, this has been among the very most common slogans, shouted at every protest. The first, "Hong Kong people, add oil!" started at the very beginning of the protests and predates them. It metamorphosed into the second, "Hong Kong people, resist!" after 4 October, when the government banned face masks at public gatherings. Then, after 8 November, when 22-year-old Chow Tsz-lok died following a mysterious fall in a car park where police were conducting a clearance operation, the slogan changed again, to "Hong Kong people, take revenge!"

"Hey, I know you!" says a skinny kid all dressed in black, black scarf pulled up to his eyeballs, black baseball cap pulled down on his forehead. Together they frame a slit of skin with two eyes in it.

"How do you know me?"

"You're from _____."

"How do you know that?'

"I'm from there too!"

I slap him on the back, give his arm a squeeze, and just as quickly as we met, we part ways.

The situation is chaotic. The police are on the move. We can't be caught off guard.

*

It was not an uncommon occurrence, kids coming up to me at the protests. I didn't know who they were; they were always masked. Sometimes I had an idea. I'd recognise a voice or the way they held themselves, especially the kids from the neighbourhood: there was just something so neighbourhood about them. Some I'd met at previous protests. Some I had no idea. They knew me, I didn't know them.

If they were from the neighbourhood, we didn't acknowledge each other back there except perhaps with a glance, an ever so slight smile. It was a blue area, and their parents almost certainly wouldn't approve of them protesting. The kids would secretly leave the house in their regular clothes, go to wherever they stashed their gear, change and *voilà,* just like Superman, they were magically transformed into protesters. It was a citywide phenomenon: teenagers from "blue" homes were joining the protests in large numbers.

The generational divide was strong. Two-thirds of people were pro-democracy, regardless of age. But the 20 to 30 per cent who were pro-Communist were disproportionately older. It was often said that if you wished for the demise of the United Front – the shadowy ecosystem of organisations and interests controlled and directed by the Party – all you had to do was wait for them to die.

Ever since the Umbrella Movement, 80 to 90 per cent of young people wanted nothing to do with the PRC, were strongly in favour of defending Hong Kong from Party intrusions, and considered the Party little more than fascists. Politically and culturally, they were entirely alienated from the regime and a Party-ruled China that it had shaped in its image, this in spite of, or more likely because of, the fact that these young Hongkongers had never known anything else, coming of age after the British handover of Hong Kong to the PRC in 1997. It would be hard to find a more damning verdict on "one country, two systems" besides, of course, the protests themselves. The Party had had the opportunity to inculcate loyalty in the generations of the future and instead had done nothing but alienate them.

This was certainly the case with university students and people in their twenties, but less so with secondary students, teenagers. Their ideas about the political situation in Hong Kong were just forming. For them especially, the protests were truly formative. They came in with eyes wide open and came out as freedom fighters.

✳

I was always a bit uncomfortable with media characterisations of the protests as student- or youth-led. Students and other young people undoubtedly played a crucial role, but the media didn't always bother with a detailed definition of exactly what that role was. And anyway, the protests were so much bigger than just youth. The people who got the protests off the ground were not the youth, but once the young people joined, things really began to move.

The first mass march of a million, on 9 June 2019, encompassed about as broad a swathe of Hong Kong society as one could imagine and included people of all different ages.

Three days later, 100,000 turned out to surround the Legco building and prevent the extradition bill from going forward. Those protesters were overwhelmingly young. But not that young. Most were post-secondary, in their late teens or early twenties. Many were university students. In this respect, the turnout was quite similar to that of the Umbrella Movement. But unlike before, many were members of the "great unwashed": they tended to be poorer and less educated, had fewer employment opportunities and lived in public housing estates. This in itself represented a broadening of the base of the freedom struggle. Over the coming weeks, young people from every corner of the city, including some of its most deprived areas, young people who were not university students, joined the protests. Arguably one of the defining characteristics of the protests was the high participation rate of youths from the scrappy, marginalised areas of the city who contributed their tenacity, toughness and fighting spirit.

It wasn't until some time later that secondary students joined in large numbers. On 21 June, at the first protester siege of police headquarters, I met three boys. They'd just finished their English oral exam that morning, had heard about the surprise protest and couldn't wait to rush down afterwards. I asked them what their classmates were thinking. They were frustrated. They said their classmates were divided between those who just didn't care about politics and those who did. The split was about equal. Among those who did care, not a single one they knew supported the regime. Everyone pretty much agreed with them: they thought the government was stupid, they couldn't stand the way the Party was trying to swallow Hong Kong. But, they said – and this was something they stressed – not many of them were willing to come out and protest.

"Don't worry," I said. "If these protests continue, they'll come out. It takes most people a while to catch on to what's going on. Give them time. Keep talking to them. Tell them about what it's like here." I turned out to be right, but I couldn't have known it then. I was just trying to reassure them. When you're 16, you feel as if tomorrow will never come.

*

There was a history going back to 2012 of teenagers being at the forefront of the freedom struggle. In that year, a large campaign broke out against the imminent introduction of a new mandatory "Moral and National Education" subject in all Hong Kong schools. The campaign was spearheaded by a newly formed group called Scholarism. Its leader was an unknown 15-year-old named Joshua Wong, the future pro-democracy icon. Scholarism grabbed public attention by occupying Civic Square, the area outside government headquarters used for protests before the government closed it in 2014. A strong coalition of diverse groups led by students, parents and teachers was formed. The movement built to a climax of upwards of 100,000 surrounding government headquarters, the first-time protesters had ever surrounded the complex. Amazingly, the government backed down. It said the introduction of the subject would be voluntary on the part of schools, its face-saving way of shelving it since few schools really wanted the subject in the first place.

That campaign was not only led by teenagers but was about an issue, their education, that directly impacted them. It made young people aware of the importance of politics in their lives and awakened their political consciousness. For most, it was the first political movement in which they'd ever taken part. And it succeeded. Many young people came out of the fight against national education with the sense that, yes, maybe they could change things for the better, though of course all we'd really accomplished was to have prevented the worst from happening.

Teenagers again played a leading role in the Umbrella Movement. In late September 2014, university students called a week-long class boycott and gathered at government headquarters to protest the Party's decision to rule out genuine universal suffrage indefinitely. On the last day of the university boycott, secondary students, led by Scholarism, joined in. Just as the week was about to conclude, the students sprung a surprise: they occupied Civic Square, the very place occupied by Scholarism in 2012. But earlier in 2014, the government had closed it to the public and fenced it in. Police arrested Joshua Wong almost immediately but didn't manage to remove the rest of the occupiers until the middle of the next day. The occupation triggered the Umbrella Movement. Less than two days later, police attacked protesters with tear gas, leading to a 79-day occupation of three different central areas of the city. At the Admiralty occupation site, next to government headquarters, an elaborate study centre was constructed right in the middle of the road. It was often full of secondary students trying to keep up with their studies while protesting.

To me, the miracle of both the anti-national education and Umbrella movements was that so many young people rebelled at all. Nothing in their upbringing and certainly not in their authoritarian education encouraged to them do so. Just the opposite: they were told to stay on the straight and narrow, to concentrate on getting ahead, not to allow themselves to be distracted or to harm their future by getting involved in something so contentious and, indeed, dangerous as politics. In protesting, they were going against their upbringing and education. And they were creating a youth culture that had resistance in its DNA.

While there was this legacy of teenagers playing a leading role in the Hong Kong freedom struggle, by the time of the 2019 protests, those from previous campaigns were already veterans in their early twenties. Few of the tens of thousands of secondary students who'd end up joining the anti-extradition protests had ever been involved in the freedom struggle before. A whole new generation was coming out to the streets, maybe the most crucial generation of all.

✴

It wasn't just kids from my neighbourhood who kept coming up to me at protests. It was all sorts. I was one of the relatively few old-timers consistently on the front lines with the youth. I didn't wear a mask – another old-timer attribute. I came from that generation for which civil disobedience, in its classic sense, was a core precept of protest: you stood up for what you believed in, which may at times entail breaking the law, you did so openly, you accepted the consequences. Showing your face to the world was a mark of your unimpeachable integrity. I understood why everyone wore masks now: young people, old people, all people regardless of age; in fact, I thought it sensible in this time of mass surveillance when police were constantly threatening crackdown, declaring just about all marches unlawful, poring over video evidence and showing up at people's doors. It just didn't come naturally to me. I had an aversion to it. It felt psychologically strange and physically uncomfortable. The very first time I ever wore a mask in my life was after 4 October, when the government banned face coverings at public gatherings, and then only out of civil disobedience. "The government has forced me to wear a mask!" I declared through my new mask. But it didn't last long. The result of my masklessness was that I was easily recognisable, the crazy guy on the front lines without mask or protective gear of any kind. As police violence increased, the frontliners' protective gear became increasingly sophisticated – gas masks, helmets, goggles and even sometimes jury-rigged body armour. And there I was "naked". I clearly didn't know any better.

Lots of kids recognised me because I'd been a teacher. Though it had been six years since I'd last worked in a school, my reputation preceded me. I'd had the brilliant idea of starting school human-rights groups. Some were still going strong and in fact providing new recruits for the freedom struggle.

It wasn't easy to get them started. Some schools were willing to allow the groups because they thought they were mostly interested in the human rights of people far away.

They had no problem with an awareness-raising campaign on maternal mortality in Burkina Faso. They thought this sort of thing could actually burnish their reputation for inculcating "global awareness" and "caring for others" in their students. But the groups turned out to be more like Trojan horses, taking on causes closer to home, in Hong Kong and in their own schools, a turn I not only supported but encouraged. What the groups were really about, from my point of view, was teaching kids how to be responsible, assertive citizens and to act politically based on their ideals.

The groups called for democratisation of school governance and, specifically, student representation on the school board. They took "human rights inventories" of their schools, producing reports that showed them wanting in more than a few key areas. The breaking point came when the groups planned an LGBT rights week at their schools to coincide with Hong Kong's annual Pride parade. Influential parents complained to school administrations, which in turned complained to my school, which in turn pressured me. I told them it was perfectly within the students' rights to organise such events. That was the beginning of my end. I jumped before I was pushed, deciding there simply wasn't a place for me any longer in the Hong Kong education system.

But the groups, now almost entirely student-driven, continued to spread to other schools. Often, they weren't officially recognised and took on something of an underground edge. Many members participated in the anti-national education movement and the Umbrella Movement.

Not long after the 2019 protests began, Communist propaganda appeared, asserting that I was "inciting" young people. I felt almost as if I were receiving a belated award:

after all, I'd been trying to incite them for years, not to violence but to rebellion. Photos of my conversation with those three boys that, judging by the angle, could only have been taken from inside of the police headquarters compound, were published in a Party-owned newspaper and circulated on Party-allied social media to substantiate the claims.

I'd always had an inherent allegiance to the young people of Hong Kong. I really believed all the clichés about the youth of today being our future, and the youth of the city in particular were the future of the freedom struggle.

As its allies died off, the Party would have to contend with the resistance of the majority of young people, today into the indefinite future. Yes, it would try to indoctrinate, intimidate and co-opt them, but the Party had failed miserably at that up to now, producing the exact opposite reaction to what it intended. It saw schools and universities as a key battleground in the struggle over the future of Hong Kong, and many of its post-Umbrella efforts to gain greater control had targeted education.

*

In Hong Kong, lack of democracy and gross income inequality went hand in hand. By some measurements, Hong Kong was the most unequal developed society in the world. In earlier decades, when the economy was growing strongly, there was enough upward social mobility to offset this structural defect. I knew many who'd grown up in public housing estates, where nearly half the Hong Kong population lived because they couldn't afford housing at market rates. They went on to university and became accountants, dentists, nurses. But as Hong Kong reached a stage approximating full development, economic growth slowed and so did upward mobility. It became harder to improve one's place in life. Class hierarchies – which had always been strongly tiered – hardened. It wasn't too much of a caricature to say that Hong Kong society could be roughly divided into three classes: masters, servants and masters' assistants (glorified servants).

The Hong Kong education system had a reputation for being fiercely competitive. Parents jockeyed to get their children into the best schools. The children were then pushed and pushed and pushed to do their best and then better. Why? Because it was an unequal and therefore a competitive society, a society of winners and losers, and parents wanted to do all that they could to ensure their children were the winners, not the losers.

The gross inequality in the society was both mirrored and perpetuated by the education system. At the top were the international schools, most of whose students were not foreign kids who just happened to be in Hong Kong for a short spell but Hong Kong kids who were born and grew up in the city. These kids were the company owners and managers of the future. The tuition for many of these schools approached that of private universities in the US. Then there were the direct-subsidy schools (DSS) – private schools, many with religious origins, that were so called because they received subsidies from the government to be affordable to the middle classes. These kids would be the middle managers of the future, the accountants, maybe lawyers and doctors. Then government schools were divided into three tiers, or bands, according to supposed academic ability. Kids who went to Band 1 schools had the same opportunities as DSS kids. Band 2 and 3 schools were for the servants of the future, the security guards and cleaners and construction workers, the ones with jobs that didn't require a university education, the mass underclass of Hong Kong workers who kept the city going and periodically returned to their 350-square-foot chicken coops in public housing estates for rest. (DSS and Band 1 kids got 700-square-foot chicken coops. International school kids got palaces in the sky.)

Needless to say, international schools were almost exclusively attended by the wealthy, and Band 2 and 3 schools disproportionately by kids much further down the socio-economic ladder. Thus, the school system largely reinforced the grossly unequal political and economic order, which in turn reinforced the unequal school system, a vicious cycle, a stitch-up all down the line.

Communist propaganda about the protests often said that Hong Kong's underlying problems were social, not political. According to this view, young people were protesting because they couldn't afford housing. That was a funny proposition considering that in the more than 800 protests of more than 14 million protesters, there was never a slogan or a sign that had anything to do with the demand for affordable housing or any other socio-economic issue. All of the demands were political. But the regime was onto something insofar as it was true that young people were protesting the basic unfairness of the system, the entire system, the political system, the economic system, the political-economic system. Because the two were virtually one.

Young people looked around them and saw no future for themselves and very little freedom. They saw that no matter how hard they worked, they would struggle for years and years and years. Economic power was concentrated in the hands of a very few. The regime monopolised political power.

What hope could be found in such an arrangement? Often I heard young people say, There will be no future unless you fight for it. Some observers considered young protesters nihilistic. What they had in mind was the "escalating violence" and slogans like, "If we burn, you burn with us". But young people didn't want to burn it all down; the gist of the slogan was that they saw the future of Hong Kong in such stark terms, they knew they had to give their all to fight for it. They would force the regime into a showdown in which it could only lose, even when it thought it was winning. The regime thought it could pulverise us with its might, could eat the young alive, but it was sowing its own doom.

✴

It was the more aggressive, confrontational actions that inspired secondary students the most: the 12 June surrounding of Legco, the 21 and 26 June sieges of police headquarters, and, perhaps more than anything else, the Legco break-in of 1 July. The more it looked like rebellion, the overthrow of the regime, the more they liked it. Then the district marches of July and August spread the rebellion to most every corner of Hong Kong and sent the message that each and every person had to take responsibility for the freedom struggle in their own community, not just turn up for a mega-march in the city centre. Protests blossomed everywhere.

As soon as they returned to school after the summer holiday, secondary students were ready to rebel. The first protest explicitly organised by secondary students was held on 22 August. On 2 September they declared a week-long strike, coordinating with university students and workers who also went on strike the same day. Dozens of protests took place at secondary schools around the city.

But teenagers soon found that there was so much pressure on them by school authorities and parents to attend classes, and the punishments for not obeying were so severe, that they developed their own ways of both going to school and demonstrating. On 23 August, a human chain protest called the Hong Kong Way was held all across Hong Kong. It was inspired by the Baltic Way protest of that date in 1989, when the peoples of Estonia, Latvia and Lithuania joined hands all along their borders with Russia to demonstrate for freedom and independence. In Hong Kong, 210,000 turned out. The event set off a chain reaction, with hundreds of smaller human chains occurring in subsequent weeks.

It was the perfect form of protest for secondary students. Human chain protests were held usually right before school, in the early morning, or right after, in the late afternoon, right outside their school or nearby. There were many multi-school human chain protests, sometimes with students from upwards of 20 schools joining together. From 2 to 6 September, the strike week, students from 42 schools took part in human chain protests. On 9 September alone, students from 188 schools formed human chains; on 12 September, 47; and on eight other days in September, anywhere between three and 20.

Altogether, over the month, students from at least 343 secondary schools took part in human chain protests in almost every area of the city, over 70 per cent of the 472 secondary schools in Hong Kong. There were no solid counts of students participating, but I estimated about 100 students per school, a total of 34,300 who joined the human chains, a little over 10 per cent of the 325,498 students enrolled in Hong Kong secondary schools in the 2018-2019 school year.

This was in addition to the strikes held within the schools and rallies held at various parks and public spaces around the city over a period of months as well as, of course, large secondary student participation in the general protests. I estimated that, in all, about 100,000 secondary students participated in the protests in some way, shape or form, about 30 per cent of all secondary students. The overall secondary student participation rate was slightly lower than the general population's participation rate of 30 to 45 per cent, but not by much. Somewhere between 2.9 and 4.4 per cent of all protesters were secondary students in a city where they made up about 4.3 per cent of the overall population.

One would have to think hard to recall another movement in which so many minors participated, especially over such an extended stretch of time. The September 2019 climate strikes in which millions participated had a very high percentage of minors, but they were worldwide and strikes in most places lasted but a day. In 1976, 10,000 to 20,000 schoolchildren participated in the iconic Soweto Uprising in the South African freedom struggle, another largely one-day event. Large numbers of minors also participated in the Arab Spring of 2011. The Syrian uprising was sparked by schoolchildren writing graffiti on a wall. The rebellions in which the highest number of minors as a percentage of the population participated were probably the first and second Palestinian intifadas. In some indication of the sacrifices they made, 332 of the 1,284 killed in the first intifada were minors, 982 of 4,745 in the second intifada.

It was in that period, early in the school year, that teenagers joined the movement en masse. All of the events were entirely non-violent, though that didn't stop authorities at some schools from threatening students with punishment or the government and police from threatening students with arrest for unlawful assembly over the human chain protests. The threats always took the form of faux expression of concern for young people. The Education Bureau also began to intimidate and attempt to punish their teachers, who were seen to be aiding and abetting their participation in the protests. In many cases, they were.

In addition to the non-violent student protests, teenagers were also increasingly joining the general protests, both the non-violent and violent, and more and more often as frontliners. This meant they were also increasingly getting seriously injured and arrested. The three victims of police shootings with live ammunition were 14, 18 and 21 years old. One 15-year-old was shot in the head with a tear gas canister and remained unconscious for a month. As of 23 January 2020, 7,165 protesters had been arrested. About 40 per cent were students; 1,170 were secondary students, 16 per cent of all arrestees. Given that secondary students made up 2.9 to 4.4 per cent of all protesters, the number of secondary students arrested was disproportionately high. Broken down by age, 1,199 arrestees were under 18, and 4,608 between 18 and 30 years old; in all, 5,807 of the 7,165 arrestees were under 30. Students in general and secondary students in particular were making huge sacrifices. Some said they were foolish to put their lives and their futures at risk. Government and police officials routinely lamented these numbers, all the while continuing to shoot and arrest them. But the students themselves were always very conscious of what they were involved in. In months of talking to hundreds of teenagers, I never met a single one who struck me as deluded. In fact, they were clear-sighted; they understood the situation very well.

✽

I often brought my daughter to the students' human chain protests. They were the only ones I would let her attend any more. The others were just too dangerous: you never knew when the police might attack. She was frustrated. As a little girl she camped out in a tent at the Umbrella Movement. She was raised on protest, and now I was telling her she couldn't go. She was a good deal younger than the secondary students. They were heroes in her eyes; she wanted to be like them when she got older. Invariably, some girls would take her under their wing and there she would stand in the chain, a head or more shorter than all the others, singing the songs, chanting the slogans.

One day we went to one of the very poorest parts of the city. It was from here the servant classes were drawn. Wide swathes consisted of little more than a forest of public housing estates. Because of the high population density, there were also many schools, schools that used to be politically quiescent; nothing but the grinding routine of survival ever happened. Until now. Now hundreds of students from 20 schools were joining hands. The chain stretched easily a kilometre up and down one of the main streets.

My daughter took her place between girls in green school uniforms. Days before, police had taken a man into an alley and kicked him. The man was a member of Protect Our Children, the group that stood on the front lines and tried their best to do just that. They wore yellow vests to distinguish themselves. When police were later asked about this kicking at a press conference, a spokesperson referred to the man as a "yellow object" of some kind. The comment went viral. The girls all wore signs that said "green object" and gave one to my daughter.

Two of the girls had a Badiucao flag. Badiucao was a Chinese artist exiled in Australia and a strong supporter of the Hong Kong freedom struggle. He even made a flag for it, a patchwork quilt of different colours modelled on the multicoloured Post-it notes covered with the dreams of citizens that were put up on Lennon Walls all over Hong Kong. No one had taken to mass producing the flag, and it was still something of a rarity on the city streets. "Where'd you get the flag?" I asked the girls. "From our teacher," they said.

I was struck by how receptive and enthusiastic the passers-by were. This was a part of town where people looked haggard, weighed down by life. Most were just trying to get by; they didn't have time for politics. And yet they cheered these young people on. Previously, a typical response might have been to look down on them: they didn't know what they were doing, they were too young to understand, they were ruining their future. But now these people saw it was the children who knew the way and were courageous enough to lead us there.

It was one of those moments when I realised how vast and deep the support for the freedom struggle was. There was such a joyous feeling on the street. It wasn't the joy of careless teenage abandon, when the rest of the world and the past and the future disappear and you live entirely, consummately in the moment. It was the joy of taking a stand and playing an important role in a cause much larger than oneself. But it was just as undiluted and powerful. If people here were supporting the youngsters, we'd turned a corner; the uprising had reached critical mass. And it was because these kids were willing to get out on the streets and bring the struggle to the districts where they lived.

Some might be sceptical of the effectiveness of a human chain protest. You come out, you hold hands, you form a long line and shout slogans and sing songs for an hour or so, and you disperse. So what? You've accomplished nothing. But when there are hundreds of those that go on for a month and more in every corner of the city and they're undertaken by the city's younger citizens who have no other motive than to defend their home and fight for freedom, it has a strong impact on the city's atmosphere. It is hard for the average citizen to remain unmoved; it prods you to decide where you stand, as you're faced with it every day wherever you go.

This was true also of the mall sing-alongs of "Glory to Hong Kong", which blossomed everywhere around the same time. These too were seemingly innocuous protests that "didn't do anything" but nevertheless contributed strongly to the spirit of the struggle, projecting its omnipresence in every area of the city and every part of people's hearts. Lennon Walls served a similar function, though of course they weren't human. They were a highly visible reality in people's daily lives, a part of the urban landscape, in the same way that advertising usually was. The student human chain protests, the mall sing-alongs, the Lennon Walls all brought the freedom struggle to the people: it was everywhere you went, in the air you breathed.

*

Running, running, running. Sometimes it seemed that was all I ever did. Running with the kids running from the police. In every area of the city. Day after day and week after week. All of those days and nights blurred together, all of those runs became indistinguishable. The protests stretched my geographical knowledge, taking me to every part of the city. I found myself in areas I thought I knew but clearly didn't and other areas I hardly knew at all, running down streets I didn't know the names of, often disoriented, following everyone else. I was always turning to those next to me and asking, Where are we going? What's the decision? What are we doing now? More often than not, the answer was, I don't know either; all of us running to we knew not where, just away. How, I would catch myself thinking, could this possibly constitute a freedom struggle, to be constantly in retreat?

Being on the front line meant being attacked. It meant becoming an expert in ordnance. I'd had rubber bullets and sponge grenades and beanbag rounds and pepper balls whiz by my head. I'd been bashed to the ground twice by clear round plastic shields wielded by charging riot police.

The first time, I saw them coming and turned to run but faced a wall of protesters that wasn't moving nearly as fast as the police coming up from behind. Even before I could turn back to see how close they were, bang! I was knocked to the ground. All those clichés about having the wind knocked out of you and seeing stars: they're true. But I knew I had to get up. Just as I made to do so, an officer lunged and grabbed my ankle, trying to pull me towards him. But he tripped over a protester lying between us and I wriggled away. Getting to my feet, I high-stepped over a tangle of arms, legs, torsos, and sidestepped batons, but the only direction I could go was back across police lines. I sneaked into a group of two dozen journalists standing off to the side. The police scanned the group for protesters. I had no camera, no press vest, an obvious interloper. It was irresponsible to try to blend in with the journalists: I endangered them. There was a long-standing pattern of police attacking reporters and claiming journalists were fake. But the journalists discretely ensured that I remained ensconced among them. If the police decided to get me, they'd have to go through them. The police barked repeatedly at the journalists to move back and give them room to make arrests. Protesters were lying face down in the street mere metres from us with police piled on their backs. The young man the officer tripped over while trying to get to me was among them. He looked straight up at me and smiled. Before long, I was able to sneak back into an alley and hide behind garbage dumpsters until the police moved farther down the street.

The second time, we were running fast down Hollywood Road through an upscale area of restaurants and bars. The police came screeching up in vans that nearly collided with us and piled out in large numbers. Bang! Down I went on the pavement, hands and forearms scraped and covered in blood. Again I'd been overtaken and surrounded. I looked up and saw the wealthy and mostly foreign-looking patrons of a nearby big-windowed restaurant motioning for me to come. I ran in and a waitress immediately ushered me back into the kitchen where I hid until the police were gone.

I'd been pepper-sprayed many times, but badly only twice.

The first time was on Halloween. A march was intercepted by police. A woman dressed in what looked like a dancer's costume from a 1920s Parisian cabaret was waving her big bum at the police while insulting them. They charged, pepper-spraying the crowd to clear us from the vicinity, smothering the woman beneath them. I got it right in the face.

Pepper spray is worse than tear gas. It hurts more and for longer, up to 24 hours. If you try to wipe it away, you just spread the burning sensation. Water doesn't help: the spray's oil-based. The only thing that provides some relief is milk. But I didn't go out on the street with milk, and the first-aiders didn't carry it either.

The second time was at the Uighur solidarity rally in December. It had been approved by police, but they attacked it anyway. Someone pulled down the PRC flag from a nearby flagpole, and the police came charging. Again, they flailed about with the pepper spray in big indiscriminate arcs. I was trying to photograph the ones who got caught, in order to alert others, and got it right in the face.

And I was someone who'd never lifted a finger against the police and never would. All because I chose to stand in the front lines, alongside the kids. Why?

I wasn't a kid myself. Far from it: I had kids of my own. I found myself, an advocate of non-violence, in situations in which people were throwing petrol bombs and setting fires in the streets. I didn't try to stop the violence; that wasn't my role. It was a choice the frontliners had made. I supported them as comrades. It would have felt entirely wrong to sit at home watching or even to stand back, allowing others to take the blows on my behalf.

I would have prevented protester attacks on civilians if any occurred in my presence, but they never did. It wasn't as if I was of much use otherwise. I could disappear tomorrow and it wouldn't make a difference. I sometimes scouted police positions and alerted others to imminent attacks, but that was hardly indispensable: people could well enough figure things out for themselves.

Though if I thought hard, I could come up with a few

reasons to be running with the kids, it really had to do with a sense of solidarity, of responsibility, to do with standing by young people. I had the quasi-magical idea that my presence might somehow lessen the blows of the police or make them think twice about carrying out excesses. I wanted to witness, so I could understand and tell others. But above all, out of obligation, duty, fondness, affection, a desire to protect even when I knew that was not in my power.

Over the months, especially from August through October and into November, as the number of really young people – teenagers, secondary students – on the front lines grew, the lessons they were learning were not the kind one got in school.

One evening, quite late – we'd been running from the police for hours and they were closing in – one of the kids came up to me and said, not without a hint of pride, "I have acquired a new skill. I want to show you."

He walked up to a Bank of China branch, took out a ball hammer, and gave the middle of a thick pane of glass a hard knock. It was about four metres wide and three tall. Nothing. He knocked again. Again nothing. He turned and looked at me, smiled, and then turned back to the glass. Another knock, this one harder than the others, and suddenly, just like that, the whole pane came down in a shower of pebble-like pieces. From a purely aesthetic point of view, it was beautiful, raining down on its maker as he dashed out of the spray, hood pulled up over his head, the glass tumbling down his back and onto the ground. He proceeded to do the same to another pane of the same bank around the corner. When he was done, he crossed the small side street, shouted for me to follow, and went around another corner. I turned it just in time to see the whole glass façade of a Starbucks come crashing down. (In Hong Kong, Starbucks is owned by a company started by the father of a pro-Communist heiress who, representing a GONGO [government-organised non-government organisation], had denounced Hong Kong protesters at the United Nations Human Rights Council. The company's cake shops had also refused to write pro-democracy messages on cakes when requested to do so by customers.) In less than five minutes, this kid had demolished three shopfronts. Just then, we heard the police charging, saw the tear gas canisters landing in the street right beside us and took off running again. I lost him in the rush.

"All it takes is a hard knock in the right place and the whole thing shatters," I later reported to a friend.

"That sounds like a metaphor," he said.

*

The skinny kid from my neighbourhood comes up beside me again. I haven't seen him for weeks. We're marching down Wylie Road now, hundreds of us.

"Why aren't you wearing a mask?"

"I never wear a mask."

"Why not?"

"Everyone knows who I am anyway. What's the point?"

"Haven't they tried to arrest you?"

"Not yet."

"Why not?"

"I guess I'm lucky. They've got too many others to arrest. Why would they bother with me?"

"They're going to get you one day. You'd better watch out. Here, put this on."

He hands me a black wrap-around scarf of a stretchy

material, the kind you pull up over your nose to right below your eyes. It goes from there down over your neck.

"Thanks. I'll take it just in case." Not wanting to reject his kind concern, I shove it deep into my pocket. In my bag, I have a dozen or so masks. People keep coming up and handing them to me. I can't imagine I'll ever wear them, but I can't bear to get rid of them. They're like souvenirs.

He rushes on ahead.

The 300 or so we've been marching with for some time are almost all young; judging by their height, some as young as 13 or 14. It's like the children's parade, I think. The longer the protests go on, the younger they get, especially these frontliners.

The trek started way down at the intersection of Nathan and Salisbury Roads, by the Tsim Sha Tsui harbour front. A protest had been called at Salisbury Garden, right along the water. It wasn't even supposed to be a march, just a rally. From the moment you even got near, you could sense trouble. Riot police in clusters were stop-and-searching almost any young person who came near. Once I circumvented them, I saw a hundred cops confronting protesters at the edge of the garden. It looked like they were intending to provoke.

There have been many other "unauthorised" assemblies the police left alone and allowed to proceed, the most recent having been the previous weekend, a march that started off right in this exact spot. What they end up doing depends on several factors, one of which is the size of the crowd: the smaller it is, the greater the chance of an attack. But it's mostly marches they attack; they don't like the idea of them spreading out around town like a virus. They're more comfortable with rallies: they can be more easily contained. So why were they being so aggressive today?

It was looking like it was going to be the first stationary protest they would try to stop before it started. The theme of the rally was support for all the "collateral damage" victims of the police attacks on protests, first and foremost journalists and ethnic minorities. Only the week before, the police had shot blue liquid containing indelible dye and a skin irritant from a water cannon truck at Hong Kong's biggest mosque, just up the road. There were no protesters anywhere in the vicinity. The government and police apologised to the imam of the now blue mosque but insisted the police had been targeting protesters, in the face of all video evidence to the contrary. Now it looked like the police were going to attack a rally to support previous victims of police attacks.

Two lines of riot police converged at the Nathan-Salisbury intersection. One line stretched across Nathan Road, the other across Salisbury, at a right angle. It was the police who blocked the road first. When people went out into the road to confront them, the police raised their blue and black flags. Then, out of nowhere, about a dozen officers in the line on Salisbury Road charged into the crowd, as if to apprehend someone. Later, some media reported protesters had thrown things at police. Perhaps that provoked the charge, but one sensed the police were just waiting for the slightest pretext. The officers who entered the crowd pepper-sprayed wildly. Protesters hit them with umbrellas and whatever else they could find. Tear gas grenades followed. Protesters were trying to run away among the cars on the road. I'd seen it coming and told the people inside to roll up their windows. There they all sat in clouds of tear gas. They'd been on their way to somewhere else but now were stuck here. Both lines of police were firing barrages of tear gas.

I followed a large group of protesters who entered

Middle Road, a side street. This was not a good idea: there was no way out. Straight ahead, there were steep, narrow stairs leading to a park. Turn left and that brought you back to Nathan Road, where the police were. We turned right and found ourselves in an enclosed cul-de-sac. I peeked out onto Salisbury Road and saw there was now a third line of police further east: we were surrounded on three sides. I shouted at the police that we had nowhere to disperse. One of them raised his rifle and pointed it at me. Maybe that was the point, to trap us.

I turned and ran back into the enclosed area where the other protesters were hopping a three-metre-tall fence topped by spikes. They'd pushed a dumpster up against it and were helping each other over the top and down the other side. Someone found two pillows – who knows from where – and put them over the top of the fence, cushioning us from the spikes. I still managed to cut my inner right calf, opening a gash several inches long. It was remarkable how quickly 300 people could get over a fence like that.

The police had already noticed we'd managed to escape and began to give chase. Seeing another line of police vans a block ahead, we veered to the east, outflanked them and ended up on the Polytechnic University campus. We'd broken the cordon.

The university was quiet and peaceful, nearly deserted. There had been a graduation ceremony earlier in the day, and a few graduates were still wandering around in their robes, taking photos. We paused there and it was then I noticed just how young most of my comrades were, younger than usual, and uniformly so. I felt as if I'd been mistakenly assigned to a children's battalion. Where were we going from there? No one seemed to know. We continued northward, and that is where I meet my mask donor on Wylie.

From there, we come out onto Waterloo Road. It appears we're trying to circle back towards Nathan to join up with other protesters there. People begin pulling up metal railings to barricade the road. Why here? Why now? Within five or 10 minutes, scouts come running fast with word that the police are on the way. We've barely got the road blocked.

The vans scream around the corner a block away, five in all. They come so fast I wonder whether there's an informer amongst us. Or did someone report us? Only later does it occur to me that we're only a few blocks away from Mong Kok police station. These cops who are experts at letting thugs beat up ordinary citizens for over a half hour without intervening are getting pretty good at what I call "the swoop". And swoop they do. The vans approach at frightening speed. Protesters scatter and flee up the street.

I'm at the back and sure I'm going to get caught, the easiest of the bunch to swoop down on. As the vans pull up alongside us, I turn and double back. Just as I do, the fifth and last van goes past, metres from me. I can see the cops inside looking at me. It's a frozen moment. They can stop and corner me easily – so many of them, so few of me – but they speed past, giving chase to the others. I turn a nearby corner and run up a side street, out of view.

I can only imagine what's happening back there on Waterloo. Once again, I feel like shit: once again, I've got away and others haven't. And these are just kids, really kids, most of them not even twenty-somethings.

I make my way towards Mong Kok, where I can see on Telegram people are regrouping. I go into a shop to hide and check the Arrested Persons Concern Group's Telegram channel. It's still too soon. But half an hour later, I check again and the photos are posted. The number arrested on Waterloo isn't nearly as many as I feared – it looks like six or seven. That means most of the 300 managed to get away. But six or seven, as ever, is still too many. There they are, pressed to the ground, wrists tied behind their backs. I enlarge the photos and see that among the arrested is, unmistakably, my friend, my neighbour, the donor of the black scarf still deep in my pocket.

When police arrest a protester, one of the first things they usually do, after they've subdued them and bound their wrists, is to strip off their mask. There he is, which is to say, there is his face. Something within me doesn't want to look, wants to turn away. It's too painful to recognise his face, the face of a boy I've been running with all these many weeks, the face of a boy I've seen grow up in the neighbourhood over the course of a decade, from just a little kid to a teenager. This moment was his future way back then at the playground where now my own children played. The face of a boy whose parents I'm sure have no clue he's here; his parents, perfectly decent people. They run a bakery, work long, hard hours, never complain, just work, the sort who've never thought about politics, tried to steer clear, keep their heads low. How shocked and anguished they'll be to learn of their son's arrest: What have the gods brought upon us, we who never wanted more than to stay out of trouble?

Should I tell them myself? I consider it a moment, then think, No, that would be giving myself away. I'll call the legal assistance hotline and report his arrest. That'll get him a lawyer, which is what he needs most at the moment.

His face is blank, expressionless. I've seen so many arrested now: some are bewildered, some resigned, some defiant, some frightened. He's none of that. He looks like he's prepared for this a long time.

A RIOTER

沒有暴徒 只有暴政

There are no rioters, only a tyrannical regime

– protest slogan

"Hey," someone in the WhatsApp group said, "doesn't this guy live here?"

Attached was a photo: a tall, skinny young man dressed in black being led away by the riot police, wrists bound behind his back. From the background, I could tell he'd been arrested on Queensway in Admiralty, only a couple of blocks away from government headquarters.

The day wasn't even over and already news like this was pouring in: who'd been arrested, what atrocities the police had committed, etc. We all pored through our Telegram channels and shared info on our WhatsApp groups, trying to keep abreast of what was going on. In those days, so much happened so quickly, one could hardly keep up.

※

It was 29 September, Global Anti-totalitarianism Day. All around the world, in dozens of cities, Hong Kong solidarity rallies were being held. All went off without a hitch except in the one place those others were showing solidarity with: here, in Hong Kong, as people began to gather in Causeway Bay in the early afternoon, police tear-gassed them.

Amid all the other abuses they'd committed, this was the first time in months of protest that they attacked a march to prevent it from starting. They'd attacked plenty of other protests that had already got under way, and, at that point, they'd denied the "notice of no objection" required by the Public Order Ordinance (POO) to all other marches for weeks (and would continue to do so until December; marches were banned for 12 weeks in all).

The organisers of the Global Anti-totalitarianism Day march had pointedly decided not to apply for a "notice of no objection" and said so clearly, figuring what was the point, they were all banned anyway; why go through the motions for an inevitable outcome? Perhaps that was what had so antagonised police that they felt they had to attack us before we'd even started. Still, as with many firsts, I was a bit shocked. Tear gas I'd eaten before, lots, just not from the protest's start.

We were just two days away from the "day of mourning", what the Communists insist on calling national day, the seventieth anniversary of the founding of the republic no less. It was said they'd do almost anything to ensure the protests would end before then. For weeks, there had been rumours and sightings of troop movements near the border, and the Party had ramped up the threatening rhetoric. Hong Kong people didn't seem nearly as worried about this as the rest of the world, perhaps because we'd got so used to the bullying and intimidation. As the date drew nearer, it became clear there was no way to put an end to the protests before then; they had a momentum of their own, a momentum that, if anything, had increased with the big day in view. All that could be done was to ban them and then attack the ones that defied the ban, preferably in such a way as to cause the regime as little embarrassment as possible. It didn't look very good to have a territory under your control in open rebellion as you celebrated all your glorious achievements, but much worse would be a straight-out massacre.

Other rumblings emanated from the authorities. It was said that the government was considering banning the wearing of face masks. Most everyone in those days covered their face when they went to protests. All knew how arbitrary and indiscriminate the regime could be, how closely we were watched, and now that all marches were banned, just for turning up, you were potentially guilty of at least one crime, unlawful assembly. The regime was criminalising protest and then threatening to criminalise you once over again for wearing a mask to a protest.

The city felt as if it were perched above the abyss.

*

Yeah, I knew that guy. As soon as I saw the photo, I recognised him; he looked like his old self. Ah Kan, my neighbour, not next door but not too far away. I saw him around now and then. We'd been through a lot together.

We got to know one another during the Umbrella Movement: we noticed each other at the protests. After Umbrella, we lived through the difficult years, when it seemed well nigh impossible to get anything started, to get anyone besides the staunch souls who were always there to come out. He was there then, always there. We'd often find ourselves riding home together on the last train late at night after a protest. We compared notes, lamented missed opportunities, our own side's weaknesses and fissures, analysed why yet again we didn't quite get the next stage of rebellion off the ground. He was one of the few in the neighbourhood as radical as I, committed; the struggle always came first.

He was a musician. He kept to himself. He had an evasive, almost secretive quality. We talked politics, but I knew almost nothing about his life, or what exactly he did to make a living. I assumed he gave music lessons.

I also knew he was a Christian. I can't remember how I knew: he never said a thing that sounded remotely Christian. I'd heard Ah Kan was a big deal in the small world of Christian music in Hong Kong. He was one of those alternative Christian types, the ones who actually live according to Christian values. In Hong Kong, one kind of Christianity was akin to an upper-middle-class status symbol, like membership in an elite club. Two of Hong Kong's four chief executives had been Catholics in a city where only a little over 10 per cent of the people were Christian. Then again, Christianity had always been an important element in the pro-democracy movement. The founder of Hong Kong's first pro-democracy party was a Catholic, and one of the three founders of Occupy Central with Love and Peace, one of the leading groups in the Umbrella Movement, was a reverend.

But by the time of his arrest, I hadn't seen him in a while. I remembered wondering whether he'd been hiding.

Not long before the anti-extradition protests kicked off, he'd been involved in protests against the imminent passage of the law to criminalise insulting the PRC anthem. That the regime thought such a law was needed spoke volumes, as did the fact that rather than attempting to inculcate a voluntary and natural affection for it or anything associated with PRC-ruled China, the regime preferred imposition, the only relationship with a people in which it was well versed.

He and a bunch of musician friends played the PRC anthem, "March of the Volunteers", in all kinds of funny ways that might be legally construed as disrespectful or insulting if the law came into effect. The centrepiece of the protest was Ah Kan sitting on a stool in a cage playing and singing the anthem in an unmistakably mocking tone.

That event now seemed a chilling omen, as I stared at the photo of him being arrested. Due to the anti-extradition protests, not only was the extradition bill eventually entirely withdrawn, but the tabling in Legco of the bill criminalising disrespect of the anthem was postponed indefinitely. (And in the meantime, Hong Kong people finally made our own anthem. But I'll leave that story till later.)

Shortly after the protests began, I saw him and made some comment to the effect of, Wow! Like, wow! And, what do you think?

He replied with some cryptic pseudo-wise comment like,

We all must work hard in our lives to be the best person we can be.

He was always in a hurry, scurrying off somewhere, being his evasive self, so I didn't get a chance to ask him what he meant but sensed he wouldn't have wanted to elaborate anyway. It was weirdly apolitical. Such a big moment and that was all he had to say? We'd both been waiting years for something like this. And he goes all mystical?

I puzzled over it for some time: Had he given up on politics? Did he not really care what was going on? How could anybody not care, especially him? Was he secretly involved in something he didn't want even me to know about? A lot of people were in those days, hatching all kinds of plans, some that would meet with less approval than others. So a lot of people were keeping quiet, becoming secretive, covering their identities, online, in real life. Maybe him too. Still, it was strange.

*

When I saw the photo of him being arrested, my first thought was, Oh, so he *is* involved after all! He hasn't opted out of the struggle. There he is, as he always was – often with me – in the past. My second thought was, *There* he is, and there I was. I had been in the exact same place as he when he was arrested, at more or less the same time on that day, the 29th. Queensway, two blocks from government headquarters.

The Global Anti-totalitarianism Day march had already been going on for hours at that point. Two hundred thousand had come out, not bad considering that it was organised online by no recognisable organiser, had not applied for and therefore not received a notice of no objection from police and had been attacked by police as people sought to gather at the start point in Causeway Bay. And still, in spite of all that, a couple of hundred thousand came. It was one of those many moments when I just stood back and regarded Hong Kong people, their courage, their tenacity, their insistence on their rights, with awe and admiration.

When the police tear-gassed those gathered at the start point on Hennessy Road, thousands who'd been waiting in the nearby side streets flooded out into the thoroughfare. And the police, who were not many in number at the time, decided to back off. The march proceeded, people walking faster than at a police-approved march, fearing they could be attacked again at any time. But police didn't attack again. It was as if they had made a half-hearted effort to scare people into not coming out and then backed off.

We marched to Central and then circled back towards government headquarters. That was what set things off; in the early months of the protests, government HQ was a frequent flashpoint. Police were charged with defending it at all costs. As we passed along Harcourt Road, police attacked with tear gas, toxic blue water from the water cannon truck, rubber bullets and sponge grenades – the panoply of "non-lethal" and "less lethal" weapons at their disposal. Hundreds of riot police emerged from Central and started moving towards us. Protesters, or at least those I was with (I later heard a good many remained in the vicinity of the HQ), retreated to Queensway. From there, it looked like police intended to continue pushing us away from government HQ, back towards Causeway Bay, where we'd started.

Protesters set an Admiralty MTR entrance on fire. Black smoke billowed up into the air. They threw petrol bombs at police lines, all of them landing in the no-man's land a couple hundred metres long between the two sides; they were intended primarily to be defensive, to maintain distance between police and protesters.

But then, rather than keeping that distance and continuing to shoot tear gas, police charged. The black-clad raptors led the way, performing snatch and grabs, dashing into the protesters, grabbing the easiest to get their hands on, and dragging them back to police lines. Ah Kan was among the victims.

So as I stared at the photo of him being led away to jail, his wrists bound behind his back in plastic ties, I had one of those "there but for the grace of God" moments: it could just as easily have been me. I was in the same place at the same time.

In a wider sense, that was how I thought about all the protesters arrested. It could just as easily have been me. Most protesters felt that way. It was why there was such strong solidarity. A kind of martyrology had also developed: the feeling that we had to persist in order to honour the sacrifices and suffering endured by so many in the movement, arrestees among them; it was the least we owed them; to give up would be to betray them. They had sacrificed and suffered on our behalf; that was something not to be forgotten at any moment. When they were arrested, it was all of us who were arrested. When they were put on trial, all of us were on trial.

When the protests started in June, I began keeping track of arrests. I'd done the same during the Umbrella Movement and in its aftermath, when dozens of pro-democracy leaders and hundreds of ordinary activists were arrested and tried, and following the police-protester clashes in Mong Kok in 2016 that led to dozens being prosecuted for "riot". So I was just continuing previous practice: I knew that one of the main ways the government would try to persecute us was through the courts – it had already become established practice, the use of the judicial system as a weapon against political enemies.

Especially after the 1 July Legco break-in, the government and police threatened hundreds of arrests. But what I could not foresee was how long the protests would go on and how many would be arrested. Even by the time of Ah Kan's arrest at the end of September, the number had climbed to about 2,000. It would continue to go up, exponentially, reaching nearly 7,000 by the end of the year. Tracking all those was more work than I could handle, but luckily, along the way, more people got on board (more on that anon). I tracked the arrests and prosecutions not only as a means of exposing their blatantly political nature and attempting to hold the authorities accountable but also because it was the least I could do to show solidarity with the persecuted.

*

As soon as I responded to the WhatsApp group message posting the photo of Ah Kan getting arrested, simply saying I knew him and confirming he lived in our neighbourhood, his ex-wife contacted me. I didn't even know he'd been married, let alone divorced. And I'd known his ex-wife all this time without knowing she was his ex-wife. Ah Ting. She was a musician too, a clarinettist. And a Christian as well. And though they were divorced, she was still loyal to him, in this respect at least; she would stand by his side throughout the ordeal.

She told me she'd been in contact with his church, which had managed to ascertain that he'd been appointed a lawyer from one of the volunteer lawyer groups that provided their services to arrested protesters.

The lawyer said Ah Kan was arrested on suspicion of unlawful assembly and possession of an offensive weapon. In his case, the "offensive weapon" was a can of spray paint. Many others had been arrested on that charge for having pliers, scissors, laser pointers, umbrellas, paint, hiking sticks and other items not usually considered weapons. It was unclear when he would be released. The lawyer had managed to talk with him once by phone and then only briefly. So many had been arrested – 146 in all that day – the police station was chaotic, the police themselves didn't seem to have a clear overview of what was going on or, at any rate, didn't see the need to bother imparting it to the lawyers representing the arrestees.

The 146 arrests on the 29th came close to breaking the single-day record at the time: 148 had been arrested during a general strike on 5 August. That record would be broken many times over in the weeks and months to come, with the 1,183 arrested in a 24-hour period on 17 and 18 November at the start of the siege at Polytechnic University (PolyU) topping them all.

By law, police were required, within 48 hours, either to release an arrested individual, on bail or unconditionally, or bring them to court to be formally charged. If police believed the defendant to be a threat to society, they could then apply to the court to have them remanded in custody. Of the nearly 7,000 arrested by year's end, most were released on bail and a few unconditionally. Nearly a thousand were formally charged in court, initiating their trials. At any one time, somewhere between 70 and 90 were denied bail and remanded in custody.

Because so many were arrested on the 29th, it looked like the police would end up keeping Ah Kan and the others pretty close to the 48-hour limit.

Ah Ting went to his flat, fed his cats and removed anything that could remotely be considered incriminating, just in case police decided to search it, something they'd done repeatedly to other suspects and arrestees.

Then, about 24 hours into their detention, she received an update from the lawyer: Ah Kan and the others would be brought straight from jail to court to be formally charged. Since 1 October was a holiday, police could extend their detention up to 72 hours, an additional day.

Then late in the evening on 1 October, a day of massive citywide protests, a day I'd spent out on the streets, part of the time hiding from police (see "Sanctuary"), I heard from Ah Ting: "They're charging Ah Kan with riot."

"What do you mean?" I asked. "I thought it was unlawful assembly and possession of an offensive weapon."

"I don't know," she said. "The lawyer just found out himself, and he knows nothing more than that."

"What about the others?"

"I don't know," she said, "but the lawyer said something about him not being the only one." No, he wasn't. After Ah Ting informed me, I heard from other contacts that in fact 96 of the 146 arrested that day were to be charged with riot. Wow, I thought to myself, it'll be the biggest trial in Hong Kong history. (It would, but would be superseded less than two months later by the 213 prosecuted for riot on 18 November.)

What had occurred? Some time in the 72 hours between the initial arrest and the court appearance nearly three days later, the Department of Justice and the police made an arbitrary decision to label what happened in Admiralty a riot and, following from that, to prosecute all they arrested there on that charge. Obviously, they couldn't have had enough time to gather sufficient evidence on all of the 96 individuals, but they were going to go ahead and press charges anyway.

✳

This wasn't the first time. On 28 July, they had arrested 44 in Sheung Wan and brought them straight from jail to court to charge them with riot. In that case, revenge appeared to be the motive. While police were focused on guarding government headquarters, protesters had gone to the Liaison Office, the Party's headquarters in Hong Kong, and defaced the PRC emblem above the main entrance with black paint. The Party was thunderously furious. Somebody had to pay. The day after they appeared in court, an extraordinary letter was leaked to the public: prosecutors who worked for the Department of Justice had accused their boss, the secretary for justice, of making prosecution decisions based on political factors. Even they were alarmed. Now here we were again; apparently, the objection of prosecutors themselves to politically motivated trials hadn't had the intended effect.

In Hong Kong, riot was a highly problematic crime. It had been my view for some time that the riot statute should be abolished. It was part of the POO, itself problematic. Human Rights Watch and the United Nations Human Rights Committee, the body of experts charged with monitoring compliance with the International Covenant on Civil and Political Rights, to which Hong Kong was party, had said for years that POO's wording was so vague that it was open to police abuse of power and that it needed to be reformed and updated to be brought into line with international standards regarding the protection of basic rights, the right to freedom of assembly in particular. Everything they'd warned about had more than come true since the protests began, with police banning protests outright, attacking peaceful protests on the slightest of pretexts, and constantly labelling protests unlawful, all under the supposed authority vested in them by the POO. The right to freedom of assembly was being unreasonably restricted and attacked as never before; indeed, it had virtually been suspended for weeks, with all marches banned. It had become exceedingly difficult to protest peacefully without fear of police attack.

But "riot" was even worse than the rest of the POO, again because of its vague wording, which left itself open to interpretation not only by police and prosecutors but also by judges who tended to be socially conservative and out of touch with society. At least unlawful assembly – which itself, I believed, should be abolished (people should not need permission from the police to assemble but only to notify them) – was relatively straightforward: Was it an unlawful assembly? Was the defendant present? Same with possession of offensive weapons: Did the defendant possess said weapon? Was it a weapon? These were the crimes for which Ah Kan was initially arrested. But riot made a person responsible for a group enterprise: after all, a single person can't riot, and how can it be argued that a person participating in a situation labelled a riot is legally responsible for the actions taken by others present? To convict for riot, the prosecution had to prove that a breach of the peace had occurred and that the defendant was somehow responsible for this. Just about anything the least bit unruly (shouting loudly, for example) could be considered a breach of the peace, and the defendant's responsibility for that was usually proven by presenting evidence that the defendant had done something violent. My position was, either charge someone with a discrete, particular, recognisably violent criminal act, such as assault or arson or vandalism, or don't charge them at all.

In the case of the Mong Kok police-protester clashes of 2016, one person had been sentenced to three years in prison for throwing a water bottle. In the latest verdict in the trial of someone prosecuted for those clashes, arrived at no less while the current protests were going on, an intellectually disabled woman was convicted of two counts of riot for digging up bricks and throwing projectiles into a fire; she hadn't even directly committed violence against a person, such as a police officer. For that, she was sentenced to 46 months in prison, nearly four years.

The maximum sentence for riot was 10 years. The conventional wisdom among protesters, especially young protesters, was that these days, you risked getting 10 years in prison just for going out to protest.

(*Ten Years* also happened to be the title of a famous dystopian film that had resonated widely shortly after the Umbrella Movement about how Hong Kong would look in 10 years under increasing Communist control. With the stepped-up repression and the hundreds on trial for riot, people now took to saying, "*Ten Years* in much less than 10 years" and "*Ten Years* is now.")

With that in mind, when I heard Ah Kan was to be charged with riot, my first thought was, Oh, fuck.

At the time of his arrest, 77 in all had been charged with riot. By the end of 2019, it would be 539. Over half of the nearly 1,000 protesters on trial by then faced the charge and about 7 per cent of the nearly 7,000 arrested.

The Party, Hong Kong government and police had taken to consistently using the term "rioter" for what I would call a "protester" as a matter of policy. The central plank in their propaganda campaign was to call protesters "rioters" and say "violence" must stop, as if the only issue raised by protesters was their own violence. In other words, the propaganda was a way to distract from the real issues, the political crisis at hand, and allow the authorities to avoid confronting them.

The first time the authorities had applied the riot label was in regard to the 12 June protest surrounding Legco and preventing it from voting on the extradition bill. The police claimed it was a riot. This was an especially outlandish assertion given that all except 100 of the 100,000 gathered that day were entirely peaceful. If anyone had rioted that day, it had been the police, who attacked the 99,900 peaceful protesters en masse. Eventually, the government walked back the claim a bit, allowing that while most had been peaceful, there had been some rioters.

But the die was cast. On 16 June, when two million people marched against the government and police brutality, the original five demands of the protests were formulated, and "Five demands, not one less" became one of the three most frequently heard chants at every protest for months on end. One of those five was that the authorities cease calling protesters "rioters", cease calling the protests "riots".

Not only were government and police not heeding that demand; they were doubling down on the use of the crime for purposes of both propaganda and persecution.

Ah Kan's case, and those of the others on trial for riot, lay at the crux of two important issues.

The first was: Who would define us? Were we to allow

our oppressor to define us, and based on that definition, to impose their will upon us, through judicial and other means, and to impose their false historical narrative of the protests as nothing but unfortunate riots? Obviously not, but our view and theirs of what was happening in Hong Kong were simply irreconcilable: "There are no rioters, only a tyrannical regime," the slogan went. The upshot of these irreconcilable views was that we were destined to engage in ongoing, open-ended, indefinite resistance until we prevailed, and we were also destined to be tried in court in large numbers. How long could people be expected to be able to keep up that resistance, especially when the whole strategy of the oppressor was to wear us down, to destroy us by a process of erosion, these very trials being a prime example of that, with the goals being to maximise the number of us in prison and impose a false historical narrative?

The second important issue was the state of the rule of law in Hong Kong. It was a truism that, unlike the PRC, Hong Kong had rule of law. This was true to a significant extent, with some qualifications, but rule of law was arguably being eroded by the use of the police as a regime militia and the use of the courts to conduct politically motivated prosecutions of opponents, especially when there were no effective countervailing measures to hold the government and police accountable for their actions. In the PRC, every organ of the judicial system was entirely controlled by the Party: the judges, the courts, the police, the prosecutors, even to a large extent the defence attorneys. In Hong Kong, this was clearly not the case, and the great majority of cases still proceeded through the courts in ways that upheld rule of law. But simply in the most literal of senses, it was not ultimately true that Hong Kong was under rule of law. First of all, the ultimate arbiter of the law in the city was not a judicial organ in Hong Kong but a pseudo-legislative organ in the PRC, the National People's Congress Standing Committee (NPCSC), which, according to the Basic Law, had the authority to overrule Hong Kong courts and had imposed interpretations and amendments to the Basic Law in the past. The NPCSC was obviously controlled by the Party, and there was not even the slightest of formal checks on its power. This also meant that the Party could choose whenever it wished to follow Hong Kong law or not. For example, it had already spent 21 years avoiding its legal obligation to introduce genuine universal suffrage in Hong Kong. The result of this was that the Hong Kong government was, from a strict legal point of view, indefinitely illegitimate. These were structural deficits in rule of law with very real consequences: the Court of Final Appeal could be overruled by the NPCSC at any time; the NPCSC could impose amendments and interpretations of the Basic Law at any time (as, for example, the anti-flag desecration law); and the Hong Kong government was not constituted according to the ultimate aim of the Basic Law. But apart from that, ever since the Umbrella Movement, the Party and Hong Kong government had aggressively prosecuted legal cases against political opponents in the pro-democracy movement. In addition to persecuting them, another purpose of this practice was to attempt slowly to erode the courts' independence so that they would more obligingly serve the regime's interests. Since 2014, the Party had repeatedly characterised Hong Kong courts as "administrative" organs and said that judges needed to be "patriotic". The trial of Ah Kan and the others and all the other riot trials and prosecutions of protesters represented a huge ramping-up of this campaign to mould the judicial system to the Party's will. There was a lot at stake besides just the fate of Ah Kan.

In the PRC, this use of the judicial system to enforce political control was disparagingly referred to as rule by law. The Hong Kong version was sometimes called "lawfare", that is, warfare by legal means.

Since the protests began, I had become familiar with quite a few cases of people being charged with riot, nearly two dozen in all. A pilot, a nurse, a soon-to-be-married couple who'd stopped to help an injured protester. Most had simply been present at an event the authorities decided to label a riot and thus were so charged. That certainly seemed to be the case with Ah Kan as well. As the young protesters said, just showing up could get you 10 years in prison. (Actually, as it turned out, of the 539 charged with riot by the end of 2019, all would be tried in the District Court – above the Magistrates' Courts but below the High Court. Cases in the District Court had a maximum punishment of seven years in prison.)

*

The morning of 2 October, Ah Ting and I left home early to go to the courthouse. On the train, she told me of a concert she was preparing. "Ode to Freedom" it was called, to mark the 30th anniversary of the fall of the Berlin Wall. In December 1989, Leonard Bernstein conducted an orchestra performing Beethoven's *Ninth Symphony* in Berlin. Instead of "Ode to Joy", he called it "Ode to Freedom" to mark the occasion of the fall of the wall. "I think Beethoven would give us his blessings," he said. (Some believed that Fredrich Schiller, the author of the poem from which

Beethoven took the text for his symphony, had originally intended to call it "Ode to Freedom", but due to Prussian censorship at the time opted for "Ode to Joy".) In a show of solidarity, soloists were coming to Hong Kong from former Eastern Bloc countries for the performance.

"So cool," I said, but what I was really thinking was, With all that's happening, the last thing I want to do is go to a concert. And as ever, I couldn't forget that just as people across Europe, across the world, were celebrating the fall of the wall and the collapse of Soviet Communism in the last months of 1989, only a half year before, the Party had massacred its own citizens in the streets of Beijing to preserve its power. And 30 years later, here we were, fighting the same regime. "Just think of the concert we'll have when we win," I said to Ah Ting, as much in response to my own thoughts as to what she'd said.

"We can use music also to urge people to victory," she said. "If it happened there, it can happen here." I was only half listening.

By the time we got to West Kowloon Magistrates' Court, hundreds were already gathered.

I had spent considerable time in this courthouse not long before: the Umbrella Movement Nine (UM9) trial had taken place here, concluding only in April, two months before the start of the current protests. In fact, there was some overlap. The first march against the extradition bill, of 12,000 people, took place on 31 March. The verdict in the UM9 trial came on 24 April. Only four days after that, the second march against the extradition bill took place. About 130,000 came, the largest protest turnout since the Umbrella Movement itself. Two of the Umbrella Movement leaders were sentenced to 16 months in prison for "conspiracy to commit public nuisance". Outrageous charges, outrageous sentences, the longest ever in Hong Kong for non-violent protest. They were sitting in prison when the current protests started, the result of lawfare. And here we were again.

I had worked for Occupy Central with Love and Peace (OCLP), one of the organisations behind the Umbrella Movement. The two people in the UM9 trial who got the longest sentences were OCLP leaders, my bosses in effect. I'd attended as much of their long trial as I could, in part because of that familiar feeling: it could just as easily have been me; these people were on trial for all of us.

That UM9 trial and this riot trial of 96 were held at West Kowloon Magistrates' Court because it was the newest, best equipped and, most importantly, biggest courthouse, the only one that could accommodate trials with so many defendants and spectators, though it still wasn't nearly big enough for the trial that would be starting today.

Ah Kan's church had arranged tickets for us. Ah Ting's admitted her to the courtroom itself, she being considered a close family member. Mine admitted me to the floor on which the courtroom was located. Without these, there were so many people lined up to get in, we would have stood no chance of getting anywhere near the court.

We met the pastor of Ah Kan's church, who handed us the tickets. He looked strikingly young. In fact, he couldn't have been older than Ah Kan himself: 30 perhaps. He was wearing a suit, as if trying to appear older and more respectable; I doubted he ever wore a suit otherwise.

Ah Ting had told me Ah Kan's church had asked her not to invite the others from our neighbourhood. The church was afraid their presence would give the proceedings a too political flavour, and this would work to the disadvantage of the defendants. I scratched my head at such caution, and when you saw the hundreds already gathered, it was clear there was no getting around the political implications of the case.

We went up to the floor where the courtroom was located. Every bit of floor space was already taken up by black-clad protesters sitting cross-legged. It looked like a sit-in. Hundreds were there. I'd never seen anything like it in a courtroom. Snaking around in the middle of the floor was a long queue for the few dozen seats in the lobby in front of the TV monitors outside the courtroom.

"How long have you known Ah Kan?" I asked the youthful pastor.

"A long time," he said. "We go way back. You know Ah Kan is a musician, right? I'm a musician too. That's how we met."

"I see."

"But we didn't like each other at first. We had very different tastes in music. He didn't like what I was doing. I didn't like what he was doing. We were rivals."

"I see."

"It was only when we formed the church that we became friends and learned to appreciate each other's music. Now we play together all the time. Well, not all the time, but often."

"That's a nice story."

"It's really Ah Kan who's the lead musician in the church. I'm the pastor. The church is really small. Just 50 or 60 people."

I knew when he said that that this was one of those alternative churches that had sprung up here and there in Hong Kong, made up of believers gathering together out of mutual affinity. I thought of them as "intentional communities". They reminded me of the original, early Christian churches, getting back to basics, dedicating their lives to values, very radical in their own way. Just the sort of place I could imagine Ah Kan.

"We don't even have a proper place to meet."

"Where do you meet?"

"In an industrial building in Chai Wan."

"Oh yeah? Which one?"

He mentioned it. I laughed. "I used to have a radio show there."

"Citizens' Radio, yes?"

"How did you know?"

"It's just down the hall from us."

"It's just about the ugliest part of town."

"Yes, it is."

"The perfect place for a real church."

"We'd like to think Jesus would feel right at home there."

"I'm sure he would," I said.

I remembered the place so well: the look, the feel, the smell of it. Surrounded by a forest of dirty grey industrial high-rises. Makeshift kitchens at street level to feed the workers. You'd take a freight elevator up to the thirteenth floor. I co-hosted a weekly radio programme about human rights around the world. "Get Up, Stand Up" we called it, after the Bob Marley song. The only show on Hong Kong airwaves focused exclusively on human rights.

Citizens' Radio was a pirate radio station. It had applied for a broadcast licence, but the government didn't ever respond to the application, not even to reject it. So it went ahead and broadcast anyway: all kinds of pro-democracy programmes, a famous youth programme, and at the time one-of-a-kind programme on LGBT rights. The station got raided on a regular basis. The broadcast authorities would arrive, accompanied by the police, confiscate equipment and arrest whoever was there. I felt offended that they'd never raided during our show. During our last show, I called the police on air several times, begging them to come. Sitting in that courtroom, in the midst of the protests, it already seemed like such a different era of the freedom struggle.

Much of what goes on in Hong Kong courtrooms is about as exciting as watching paint dry, and just about as difficult to discern. The initial court hearing, or "mention", in a protest-related case was usually just to set the next court date, which the judge decided based on how much time the prosecution requested to gather evidence. Bail was also discussed and, if bail was granted as it was in all but 8 per cent of the protest cases, bail terms were set. In most cases, prosecution had no objection to bail, so we expected Ah Kan and the others would be free to go home by the end of the day. But exactly when that would be was hard to say. There were, after all, 96 defendants, and bail had to be discussed for each of them individually.

This was assembly-line justice, I thought, but then that was a somewhat misleading term: it implied a certain degree of speed and efficiency whereas this riot trial would, more likely than not, go on for more than a year, hanging over all the defendants' lives as they tried to go on living normally. It was often said that a trial was part of the punishment, a punishment before the verdict, due to its length, its cost, the mental toll it took and the lack of certainty regarding when it would end and, most importantly, its outcome.

Along with hundreds of others, the pastor and I watched proceedings on a TV monitor outside the courtroom. I could stay only the morning, having to leave long before Ah Kan was brought before the judge. Indeed, by the time I left, the lawyers were still in preliminary discussions, and no defendant had even entered the courtroom.

Ah Ting stayed right until the end. The hearing went on until after midnight. One of the main decisions made was to split the trial in two, between two courts and two judges. One trial would be for Ah Kan and the 51 others arrested on Queensway; the other for 44 arrested on Harcourt Road, nearest government headquarters. All the defendants, including Ah Kan, had been bailed, but when she contacted me, between 12.30 and 1am, she was still at the courthouse waiting for Ah Kan to come out: there was apparently a lot of paperwork for the 96 defendants to sign before they all could be released.

On my way out of the courthouse at noon, I came down the escalator and was astounded to see hundreds waiting in another snaking queue in the large atrium at the centre of the building. That was in addition to the hundreds sitting on the floor outside the courtroom above. Of course, with 96 defendants, one would expect there'd be several hundred spectators in attendance, just counting family and close friends. But this went way beyond that. I handed my ticket to the young man waiting at the front of the queue and apologised to his two friends that I didn't have additional ones for them.

The massive outpouring of solidarity became more apparent as I exited the building and saw that, strewn all about the area, hundreds of supporters were gathered, most sitting cross-legged on the ground. Most of those in the atrium would never manage to get into the courtroom or even to the floor where it was located, and of course these people outside weren't even trying. They couldn't get anywhere near the court and had no direct access, such as the TV monitors, to what was going on inside. They were there simply to show their support.

These people were like the outer circle of concentric circles of support for protesters on trial. At the very centre, arguably, apart from their family and friends, were the lawyers who represented the protesters. There were hundreds of volunteer lawyers. Some worked in their personal capacity. Some were part of networks of volunteer teams set up by organisations like Civil Human Rights Front (the group that also organised the huge mass marches) and Civil Rights Observer. Many law firms, including those working primarily in corporate and commercial law, had set aside a certain number of *pro bono* hours to protester cases and allocated in most cases their most junior members to represent the protesters, a task most young lawyers took on with alacrity. It was really the best of law as a calling rather than just a relatively lucrative profession.

Many lawyers took on so many cases that they simply couldn't afford to do it all for free. By the time of the second mass march, of two million, on 16 June, the 612 Humanitarian Relief Fund had been set up to raise funding for legal support for all prosecuted protesters. It was named after the date, 12 June, when 100,000 peaceful protesters surrounded government headquarters to prevent Legco from proceeding with the extradition bill and were attacked en masse by the police. At the 16 June march, it raised tens of millions of Hong Kong dollars in donations, and by the end of 2019 would hit the HK$100 million mark, enough to ensure legal representation of every protester who needed it for the foreseeable future. On top of that, another organisation, Spark Alliance, which helped arrested and prosecuted protesters, had raised HK$70 million.

This work was part of the overall infrastructure of the movement. It was what made it strong, resilient and sustainable over the long term. It took the regime some time to realise the importance of this immense resource. When it did, it couldn't abide it. On 19 December, police arrested four members of Spark Alliance for money laundering and froze its HK$70 million in funds intended to help arrested and prosecuted protesters. It was the first time ever that a non-governmental organisation had been hit with money laundering charges; indeed, few were ever arrested for money laundering, full stop. From what the police said, no one could make head or tail of their case. Money laundering usually had to do with taking dirty money and laundering it somehow. Spark Alliance took money collected from donations and used it to help protesters. If the accusation was that Spark Alliance was somehow misusing the money, negligent in its fiduciary responsibilities, surely that couldn't be a matter of money laundering. Whatever the case, the arrests were widely perceived as a political attack on the movement, and when over one million marched on 1 January, 13 days after the Spark Alliance arrests, millions more dollars in donations streamed in to both Spark and 612.

Spark Alliance and other organisations also helped prosecuted protesters find work. It was often said that having a criminal record could make getting a job more difficult, and these organisations made sure that wasn't the case. Many arrested and prosecuted protesters ended up working for "yellow" businesses – those in explicit support of the protests, part of the "yellow economic circle" that protesters encouraged one another to patronise and support.

There was also an array of churches and social workers that helped prosecuted protesters to hook up with other services, whether psychological support or loans or material items they couldn't afford.

Then there was the Arrested Persons Concern Group (APCG). This started out organising supporters to go to trials, with the goal of ensuring that no protester would be left without support, no one would be forgotten. Sometimes dozens showed up, sometimes hundreds. Because Ah Kan's trial was the biggest in Hong Kong history, because the arrests had just occurred, and because all the defendants were being charged with riot, thousands showed up. But that wasn't always the case; sometimes no more than a handful would come to individual trials of unknown protesters without connections. As the police ramped up protest arrests, APCG also took to providing breaking news on its Telegram channel of arrests, often moments after they'd occurred, with photographic and video evidence. This was to alert lawyers, family and friends and to ensure that no one simply disappeared. As of the end of 2019, that channel had 140,000 followers, making it among the most followed protest-related channels.

This was because arrests touched most everyone involved in the protests and resonated in the wider society as well. Just think of Ah Kan: there were his fellow protesters, musicians and congregants as well as those in the pro-democracy WhatsApp group in the neighbourhood where he lived, who all cared deeply about his case. That's a couple of hundred people in all, at a minimum. Then think of the nearly 1,000 protesters prosecuted as of the end of 2019 and imagine that there are some 200 or so related to each protester in some way or another. That's 200,000 right there, and there were bound to be more. The trials, one of the government's main ways of attacking the movement, were in effect one of the many forces fortifying a culture of resistance, forcing us to improve our networks and ways of doing things entirely outside of the regime's control. Even some who were initially hostile to the movement became more sympathetic when people they knew personally were put on trial. I liked to think the government, which used prosecutions as a key element in its crackdown, was actually slowly but surely laying the foundation for its own demise.

Thinking about the turnout at the opening hearing of the trial and this vast network of support and solidarity behind the defendants, I couldn't help but feel gratified as I walked away from the courthouse. I was so lost in my thoughts, it took some time to realise that I was walking along a hedge bordering the street, on the other side of which was a long line of police vans. I stopped and peered through the foliage, counting seven in all. What was going on? What could they be up to? As I came near Ying Wa College, a secondary school a couple of hundred metres from the courthouse, I saw students standing near the gates, looking out.

"What's going on?" I asked, motioning to the vans.

"We don't know," one said. "We just came here to have a look."

"You know what happened this morning?" another asked.

"The arrests?"

"Yeah," he said. "Right out there where you're standing. Two students arrested for playing 'Glory to Hong Kong' on a loudspeaker."

"Incredible. What's going on inside? Are you guys on strike today?" The day before, a police officer had shot an 18-year-old secondary student at point-blank range. It was still uncertain whether he would survive. Across the city, at hundreds of secondary schools, students were striking in protest.

"Yeah, a couple hundred of us. We're all sitting around the basketball court."

"I guess the police vans are meant for the courthouse. There are thousands gathered there," I told the students. "It must be making the cops nervous."

I walked towards the intersection that separated me from the MTR station. Heading out into the pedestrian crossing and passing to the other side of the wall-like row of police vans taking up a whole lane of the road, I came face to face with a police officer holding a rifle. I couldn't believe it. I just stopped in the middle of the crossing and stared at him.

He motioned with the rifle strapped to his shoulder. "Move along." I kept staring at him. "What are you looking at? Move along," he repeated.

I usually tried to be as disciplined as possible around police. I wasn't one of those who shouted obscenities, insults and curses at them, perhaps because there were plenty doing that already. I usually refrained from saying anything at all unless I felt there was a specific issue that had to be addressed. But now I just burst out: "What the fuck? You're standing in the middle of a fucking road with a rifle, right next to a school, the day after you guys shot an 18-year-old student. Are you people out of your fucking minds?"

"What? You want me to use it?" he said, pointing the rifle at me. "Try me, you piece of shit."

He started walking towards me. The light had changed but the traffic wasn't moving; we were right in the middle of the road.

I felt a tug on my arm, pulling me away towards the other

side of the road. "Are you out of your fucking mind?" my rescuer said under his breath. "Don't you know what he's holding?"

"No," I said.

"That's a fucking MP5."

"A what?"

"A sub-machine gun."

"Oh." I'd thought it was a tear gas rifle.

*

The next hearing in Ah Kan's riot trial took place nearly three months later, on 23 December.

Ah Kan happened to be on the same early morning train as I. Meeting him there reminded me of all the times over the years we'd end up taking the same train together, except then it was on the way home late at night from protests. He was his usual jittery, ill-at-ease self, but he also seemed to have accepted the role of defendant and grown comfortable with it. He understood absurdity – the political absurdity of Hong Kong's situation, the absurdity of injustice – and so, to a certain extent, he relished confronting it or found it fitting that after all these years, he was coming face to face with it in the guise of the trial.

"How are you feeling?" I asked.

"Fine."

"Do you need anything?"

"No, I'm fine."

We both leaned back in our seats in the mostly empty train. It was still too early for rush hour.

"Ten years is a long time," I said, seeing if I could prod him to express himself a bit more.

"Yes, it is."

"But you didn't do anything."

"No, I didn't, but it doesn't matter; it's a joke."

So much for our heart-to-heart. I'd heard him use those same words several times of late: "It's a joke." Usually with arms held up to the side in a gesture of "but what can you do?" "It's a joke" really seemed about the only thing he had to say about what was happening to him.

The crowd wasn't nearly as big as at the first hearing, but there were still several hundred people. A dozen from the neighbourhood WhatsApp group showed up this time, even though not much was expected to happen. I was pleased that Ah Kan was probably one of the best supported defendants there, though he seemed a bit embarrassed by so many patting him on the shoulder and making encouraging comments.

The prosecution asked for a 12-week extension to gather evidence. The many defence lawyers protested. At the initial hearing in October, there'd been some debate on whether to schedule the second hearing eight or 12 weeks from then. Twelve weeks had been decided on, to give the prosecution adequate time to gather evidence and avoid further delays. Now here it was 12 weeks later with the prosecution asking for an additional 12 weeks. That meant the trial proper wouldn't even get started until 24 weeks – six months, half a year – after the initial hearing.

As at the previous hearing, I stood next to Ah Kan's pastor. During a break in proceedings, we made small talk. Thinking that he as a musician might be interested, I mentioned I was compiling all of the videos I could find of people singing and playing "Glory to Hong Kong": people in malls, church choirs, buskers, a singer in a jazz club, a man serenading prisoners outside a prison, protesters on the street, on sound systems blaring out into the street from shops, the list went on and on, endless versions, endless permutations, the tune becoming part of the air surrounding us, anchored in our souls.

Since it had come out in August, published on YouTube by an anonymous composer who went by Thomas dgx yhl, the song had garnered millions of views in different versions and been performed countless times in a variety of styles. The lyrics were the result of discussions Thomas dgx yhl had had on LIHKG, the Reddit-like forum especially for young protesters, and incorporated the major protest slogan "liberate Hong Kong, revolution of our times". The song had become the heart of the sing-along protests that occurred in shopping malls throughout the city and was inevitably heard at virtually every protest.

It was the movement's anthem. I called it Hong Kong's national anthem; Hong Kong had no other, and its people responded to this with great emotion, unlike the PRC anthem that was imposed upon the city. The PRC one was played at government events and sung in a language, Putonghua, that was not the native tongue of 90 per cent of Hong Kong people. Most were indifferent to it. To the extent it excited emotion at all, more likely than not it was hostility and resentment.

When people sang "Glory to Hong Kong", you could see how much it meant to them. They did it with conviction. It expressed their deep attachment to the city. Their patriotism. It seemed to me part of what I considered "the birth of a HK nation", the consciousness that we were a separate people, with a separate history, a separate language, a separate culture, a separate identity and the pride and love we felt about that. And it was a great song, powerful to sing, especially together with others; it bound us together, made us one.

For me, I told the pastor, it represented nation-building. Not intentional but spontaneous, organic. No one said, Let's build a nation; this is how we go about it. People just did it; it arose out of a deep desire. This is why I thought putting all those versions together was important: they were one of the best testaments to the spirit of the time. It was a way of showing how the Hong Kong nation came into being and how widespread this phenomenon was across Hong Kong society.

He leaned towards me and whispered, "Let me tell you a secret."

"What's that?"

"Ah Kan and I played on the orchestral version of 'Glory to Hong Kong'."

"You mean the one where the orchestra and chorus are all dressed in protest gear?"

This was the most famous and the most widely played version of the song. It came out less than two weeks after Thomas dgx yhl's original. Somehow in that short period of time, a full orchestra and chorus were assembled, and a stunning professional-quality video of their performance was produced. The musicians played in full protest gear: helmets, goggles, masks, black shirts. I'd heard they'd all taken a vow of secrecy, to not tell anyone else they'd participated.

"Yes, that's us."

"Wow, cool. You guys were making history."

"You know, no one's supposed to know who took part. It's supposed to be top secret."

"Yeah, I know."

"So don't tell anyone else."

"I won't."

When the hearing resumed, the judge granted the prosecution's request. Just like that, the hearing was over.

"See you on 13 March."

✳

I later watched the video again to see if I could recognise Ah Kan and his pastor. Even after several viewings, I couldn't be sure. But I thought I caught a glimpse of Ah Ting. I had to pause and rewind the video several times. I could tell by her glasses, the shape of her nose and the fact she was playing a clarinet.

The next time I saw her, I asked.

"That", she said, "I am not at liberty to divulge."

"Everyone's so goddamn secretive around here," I said in mock disgust.

To which she just flashed her typically beatific smile.

What she really wanted to tell me about was her recent concert in the middle of the wilderness. (Yes, in tiny urban Hong Kong, 50 per cent of the territory is green, making the half where people live even more densely populated.) It was a duet for clarinets, the other clarinettist being one of her closest friends. It had taken over a year to prepare. Especially challenging was getting the permission and cooperation of the authorities, since the concert was held in a so-called country park (Hong Kong's version of a national park) administered by the government.

But though the bureaucracy was a hassle, what worried her most was the monkeys. They were very aggressive pests. She feared they would attack the spectators. A friend had told her they'd even learned to target people's wallets because they'd seen the wallets being used at a nearby cemetery to get drinks from vending machines – you just pressed the Octopus card in your wallet up against the sensor and *voilà,* the drink dropped out of the machine. Like magic. Monkey magic. The monkeys stole the wallets to get drinks.

As it turned out, the concert went splendidly. Ah Ting couldn't have been more pleased. But at the end, just after the encore, as if it had been waiting for just that moment, with the timing of a musical genius, sure enough, a monkey made off with a woman's purse.

"But the strangest thing was my own reaction," Ah Ting said. "I hid it from everybody. In that moment, I was the happiest I could ever remember being. Happy isn't the right word. Joyful. I glowed with joy. It was as if everything suddenly came together. The monkey taking the woman's purse triggered it. It was the moment I'd been dreading, but when it happened, it was like a release, a liberation. I saw and felt and heard so many things at once, and they all blended together. It was like its own symphony. All the confusion and fear of recent months vanished. I remembered that exact feeling, that mixture of elation and terror running through the corridors of Legco on 1 July; Ah Kan's trial; all of the bad moments of our marriage when I just felt like giving up on everything, even on life – they now seemed just the way things had to be; our performance of 'Ode to Freedom', which was thunderous, and I still resent the fact you didn't come, it was dedicated to the protests, you know; and then the sound of my clarinet together with my friend's in the stillness of that beautiful wilderness; and overlaid over all that, a voice that seemed to be the monkey's voice, the monkey that by now was in the upper branch of a tree holding the purse and looking down on us all with scorn, repeating over and over, 'There are no rioters, only a tyrannical regime.'"

When I got home, I listened to Bernstein's performance of "Ode to Freedom". Really listened to it. Cranked up loud. So loud that if Ah Kan had been at home, he probably could have heard it, booming out across the neighbourhood. Of course, like most people, I'd heard "Ode to Joy" countless times, to the point where the music became kitsch, cliché. My child could play the melody on the piano. But this was the first time I really listened to it, lying on the floor, staring at the ceiling, the walls vibrating with sound, and I understood, truly understood, what Ah Ting had been trying to tell me on the MTR train going to Ah Kan's initial hearing: "Ode to Freedom" was the most beautiful music on earth.

THE SIEGE

民不畏死奈何死懼之

If people are not afraid to die,
it is of no avail to threaten them with death

– protest slogan derived from the Dao De Jing

As soon as I got there, I thought, This is a trap.

The call had gone out early that day, 17 November, a Sunday: Polytechnic University, known locally as PolyU, needed reinforcements; the protesters there were under fierce police attack.

✻

This was only days after protesters at another university,

Chinese University of Hong Kong (CUHK), had come under what up to then was the heaviest police attack yet, on the 12th. It went on for hours, from around midday until deep into the night. Metaphors of war were often used to describe the Hong Kong protests, and I tried my best to avoid them – I found them thoughtless and inexact – but that night in particular really did look and feel like war: tear gas blanketed the "battlefield"; it hung in the air for hours. Fires, set by protesters as barriers against police charges, raged. Loud booms filled the dark night, punctuated by the rat-a-tat of rifles shooting rubber bullets, sponge grenades, beanbag rounds. First-aiders ferried injured protesters away from the front line on stretchers or dangling in their arms.

The only things distinguishing the CUHK siege from war were the lack of live ammunition and the intention to kill. The police shot copious amounts of ordnance with non-stop intensity: by the end of it all, 2,330 tear gas canisters, 1,770 rubber bullets, 434 beanbag rounds and 159 sponge grenades – the heaviest one-day use of weaponry yet in five months of protests. Shot at students. Defending their university. Whom the police called rioters. Because they returned fire. With home-made petrol bombs. All fought over a bridge, another warlike aspect of the siege. The bridge was one of the few public access points to the sprawling campus, set in an area not far from the Chinese border that's about as close to rural as Hong Kong gets.

Watching the scenes that day, I had the feeling that there was no way back for the Hong Kong police. Yes, abuses had been rife up to that point, but a Rubicon had been crossed with the assault on CUHK: no longer could the police be considered a law enforcement agency, if a flawed and abusive one. The force was being used by the CCP as a proxy, a militia to put down an uprising, and had become a party to civil strife, if not civil war. People had already been calling for the complete disbanding of the police. In my bones, at that moment, I felt that was absolutely necessary. Whatever if anything might replace it, the police force as currently constituted had to cease to exist. Of course, the only way to bring that about was democracy – full civilian control over the force, a force that served the people, not their oppressor. This feeling, that we had passed the point of rupture, would only grow in the coming days and weeks.

As with PolyU five days later, the call went out for reinforcements, and many heeded it. I was desperate to go, but by the time I saw how urgent the situation had become, it was dark, and CUHK was on the opposite side of the city. So I watched until the siege subsided after midnight and waited until the next day.

I headed across town early, knowing that by that point, transport links to CUHK had been all but cut off. Most of northern New Territories (NT), where CUHK is located, is separated from the rest of the city by a mountain range. The University MTR station, next to CUHK, had already been closed the previous day, as had the stretch of highway spanned by the bridge that was at the heart of the battle. But then MTR closed all of the East Rail Line connecting New Territories and the rest of the city. Most bus routes were either entirely suspended or so significantly delayed as to be as good as suspended. In effect, there was no way in by public transport, the way the vast majority of Hong Kong people got around.

I went out to the Tai Po Road, one of the few major roads to go over the mountains (as opposed to through them – it was forbidden for pedestrians to enter tunnels). On the way,

I stopped at a makeshift supply depot on a Mong Kok street to pick up as many supplies as I could carry and loaded them into a large backpack, mostly warm clothes and first-aid supplies. On the Tai Po Road, still in the urban area of Sham Shui Po, I tried to get a taxi, but every single one that passed was already occupied.

Private vehicles weren't stopping either. Hong Kong had no culture of hitch-hiking, but still, Where was the solidarity? I wondered. Couldn't people see this was a time of emergency? Maybe Hong Kong people were more selfish than I thought. Maybe I'd romanticised and exaggerated their outpouring of solidarity during the protests. I was clearly a protester, dressed all in black; anyone could surmise where I was going. In fact, I worried about getting stopped by the police.

I was about to lose heart when I met a young man carrying a huge backpack that looked several times the size of mine. He was obviously heading to the same place. He said he'd already contacted several taxi dispatchers who all said the same thing: You'd get there quicker walking than waiting for a taxi. The lack of public transport as a result of the protests, not only to New Territories but across the city, had immensely increased demand for taxis.

And so, walk we did. Twelve kilometres over the mountains to Fo Tan, a nondescript so-called new town in the New Territories. I basically thought of these new towns, dotted around the city, as dormitories for the low-wage servant classes. They came out to work for their masters as security guards, cleaners, restaurant workers, and then returned to their chicken coops. I'd never been to Fo Tan before. So many events in the protests had exposed me to parts of the city of which I was almost entirely ignorant.

I was just following my "guide", who went by the name of Adam. He was actually a marathoner and a trail runner who'd finished the impossibly rigorous Oxfam Trailwalker 100-kilometre race through the very mountains we passed and frequently biked the route we were taking. His plan, which I freely assented to since I hadn't a clue what to do and was feeling very much the city boy, was to rent bikes in Fo Tan for the rest of the three-kilometre trip to CUHK. Near the closed MTR station were several bike shops, the bicycle paths of New Territories being, under normal circumstances, a tourist destination.

A man came up and whispered to us to follow him. He took us down winding alleyways to a bike shop several hundred metres from the station, so hidden I couldn't imagine how it got any business. "Here are your bikes," he said, not only to us but also to the dozen or so others gathered there, all with backpacks, all obviously going to the same destination. Then he hopped on a bike himself and said, "C'mon, I'll show you the way."

It all happened so fast, it took me a moment to realise, Aha, this man has done this before. It felt like some sort of underground railroad. Like us, the others came from elsewhere in the city, but we talked very little, just nodded and shared smiles of complicity. Among other things, we were all well aware any of us could be an undercover cop.

Our guide had to keep stopping and waiting for us. Along the way, we passed a secret supply station. "Those of you going back and forth", he said, "can leave your supplies here. They'll be picked up and transported to the destination. Most of these supplies come from other places in NT, especially Sha Tin. People drive in and drop them here." Lots of people spent the whole day shuttling back and forth between other points and the supply station, between the supply station and the university campus. After we dropped our first loads, Adam and I would ourselves make several trips. We continued onward. Before long, the guide pointed, "It's right up there. I'll leave you here. Be careful," and he was gone.

We'd reached the perimeter of the campus. Hundreds of people were bringing supplies in. It was an impressive, massive operation. Adam and I took our bikes further, past the MTR station, which was entirely impassable, having been barricaded by protesters to prevent police from using it to cross into the campus. Near Bridge No. 1, we lifted up the bottom of a chain-link fence and pushed our backpacks, our bikes and ourselves underneath it. Bridge No. 1 was also barricaded, but there had been no fighting there. We climbed the barricade, entered the campus, dropped off our supplies and had a look around.

Bridge No. 2 was charred black from all the fires the night before; the air had a burnt smell. There was no sign of police. Anywhere. They had entirely backed off. Of course, everyone was expecting their return and preparing for it. There were copious supplies. The generosity of Hong Kong people was astounding. The protesters had everything they needed and could have held out for a long time. There was a big petrol bomb factory out in the open, and another area where bricks were being dug up and stacked in high walls. (There were also buckets and buckets and upside-down umbrellas full of spent tear gas canisters, shot by police the day before, that someone had gone to the trouble to collect.) As it turned out, the police never did return. On Friday the 15th, three days after the police assault, protesters left the campus. The university announced classes would end early and not resume until the new semester, set to begin in January.

*

Unlike CUHK, PolyU was right in the middle of the city. Tension there had been simmering nearly a week, but it wasn't until the police arrived in large and increasing numbers over the weekend of the 16th that it reached crisis point.

It all began on Monday morning, 11 November. Or maybe three days before that.

On 8 November, Chow Tsz-lok died. He was a 22-year-old university student. Four days before, he'd fallen from one floor to another of a parking garage in Tseung Kwan O, where police were conducting a clearance operation during a protest. The exact circumstances of his fall remained mysterious: Did he deliberately jump? Did he trip and fall accidentally? Was he pushed? Protesters immediately suspected police involvement. Police denied any. Security camera footage publicly released by the parking garage owner didn't capture the fall. Tsz-lok was unconscious from the moment he was found and never regained consciousness.

His was the first protest death that had occurred in relation to police operations. (There had been some protest suicides.) What the city had been dreading had occurred: the first protest fatality. It seemed almost inevitable: for weeks people had been waiting for the other shoe to drop. Police had thrice shot protesters at close range with live ammunition. In one case, a police officer shot a young man in the upper abdomen. On video, it looked like certain death. But the bullet miraculously passed between the victim's heart and lung and came to rest millimetres from the spine. He survived and was recovering. It was Tsz-lok's fate to be the first.

There was a huge outpouring of grief and anger. People had been storing it up. The death triggered the release. Throughout the weekend, hundreds of thousands attended vigils and protests. Disruptive actions were called for Monday, under the name Operation Dawn.

*

Quite early that morning, I rushed over to PolyU after hearing tear gas had already been shot. Protesters had gathered at the campus and gone out from there to block surrounding streets. Police chased them back onto campus and fired tear gas at them. PolyU thus became the first university campus attacked by tear gas, by a day; the CUHK siege didn't begin till the next.

By the time I got to PolyU, things had quieted down; police were nowhere to be seen, and protesters had begun to use the campus as a safe haven from which they'd venture out on forays and then return.

On the way there, I had been sent a video of a cop shooting a young black-clad protester at point-blank range in Sai Wan Ho only moments before. I showed the students at PolyU the video. It had a chilling effect. This was only three days after Chow Tsz-lok had died, and here the police were shooting a kid, not for the first time, a kid who had no weapon, a kid who wasn't even attacking the cop. It looked as if the cop had simply panicked. In remarkably little time, the officer was identified and information began circulating online about him and his daughter on social media. Having been a victim of doxxing myself, along with my children, I implored protesters to cease doxxing, especially the daughter.

Protesters had already set to work barricading all of the main entrances to the campus. They hoisted the "liberate Hong Kong, revolution of our times" flag on the flagpole. They smashed the glass panes of the building just off the campus central square and spray-painted slogans like "Give me liberty or give me death". I thought to myself, A lot of people don't believe the kids really mean those slogans; they think they're just acting tough, playing at being revolutionaries. But look at the shooting this morning, a little more than an hour ago. It wasn't an exaggeration to say that being out on the front line, one was constantly at the edge of death.

The Operation Dawn actions ended up paralysing much of the transport network for the rest of the week, with roads blocked and MTR lines down or delayed. By Wednesday, the third day of the operation, PolyU protesters had shut down the Cross-Harbour Tunnel, one of the main links between Hong Kong Island and Kowloon. The tunnel's Kowloon entrance was right next to the campus. It would remain shut for more than two weeks, all through the ensuing police siege. It was this act, the tunnel blockage, that probably more than anything else led the police to force a showdown on the campus. The way they went about it, however, had to do with their apparent takeaway from the CUHK siege: you can't let up; you have to go after the rioters until you've neutralised every last one. At CUHK, after the pleas of the university head and many other eminent personages of the sort who were either themselves members of the small circle of elites used to controlling Hong Kong or whom the elites at least listened to, police had dropped the siege.

That Friday, the fifth day of road blockages across the city, including around PolyU, some pro-CCP anti-protesters began to clear barricades. On Saturday morning, when they showed up at PolyU, protesters came out from the campus and told them to stop. They didn't. Protesters threw bricks at them. The police arrived and fired tear gas. The police could have decided to withdraw after that, as they had earlier in the week, but they remained. Things escalated from there.

The assault reached its climax on Sunday, not long after I arrived. I hadn't been there for a couple of days, and, as I said at the top, as soon as I got there this time, I thought, This is a trap. I'd always been a bit claustrophobic: in every situation, I looked for an escape route. At the protests, that could be an advantage: I was always trying to think about 10 steps ahead of the current moment. The trait dovetailed with the de facto "be water" philosophy. But the sense of PolyU being an imminent trap was especially intense: I immediately had the urge to flee. Perhaps it was the shadow of the CUHK siege. Perhaps it was an apprehension of the hardened mood of the police. Perhaps it had to do with the way the protesters were digging in.

The PolyU campus is large and spread out. If anything, what was peculiar about police actions was that, rather than surrounding the campus, they were attacking it at only one point, near the junction of Chatham Road South and Cheong Wan Road, a bit like their fixation on Bridge No. 2 at CUHK. The campus was far from surrounded, anything but, yet my premonition wouldn't go away.

The siege of CUHK had been the first time in all the months of protest that protesters had stood their ground and defended territory, the diametric opposite of "be water". No one had planned it that way, thought it out from strategy; after all, we were leaderless. Like so much else, it was something we just fell into. Universities were regarded as citadels, almost sacrosanct, especially by students, and many of the frontline protesters were university students: they had to stand up and defend what was theirs.

In their pursuit of protesters, police had increasingly been entering shopping malls, where many gathered to sing protest songs and some also vandalised pro-Communist businesses. They'd also gone onto other private property such as housing estates. Such intrusions had previously been considered extraordinary. Now, after shopping malls and housing estates, universities were next. All of Hong Kong was becoming one big police state. Police said they were justified in going anywhere they needed to in hot pursuit of criminals.

There had been clashes not only at CUHK and PolyU but also the University of Hong Kong, Hong Kong Baptist University and City University of Hong Kong. It had to stop; you couldn't just let police invade everywhere. Or so went the thinking, or, maybe more accurately, the sentiment. Maybe that was the root of my premonition that PolyU was a trap in the offing: I was as worried about the mood of the protesters as the police, the idea that there was some glory to be had in valiantly defending what was ours.

The situation at the junction of those two roads flanking the campus was peculiar. Rows of frontliners had set up barricades. Police brought in two water cannon trucks and two armoured trucks. The water cannon trucks would take turns, coming forward some dozen metres, showering blue liquid containing indelible dye and skin irritant over the frontliners while other police fired tear gas, and then retreating.

The frontliners were so used to this that the attacks hardly made a dent in the lines. They wore full-length plastic rain ponchos. They responded with petrol bombs, lots of them. The no-man's land between police and protesters was continually strewn with little petrol bomb fires.

This series of events repeated itself in a pattern that went on for several hours. The frontliners would get soaked, go back to campus, strip, shower, scrub off the toxic blue dye, dry off, change and return. Eventually the campus's red brick walls turned blue from being sprayed so much by the water cannon truck's blue dye. What did the police think they were doing? Softening up the protesters? Wearing them down? Trying to soak the petrol bomb supplies with water so they wouldn't ignite?

But there was a very large supply of petrol bombs. Most were stored on the campus itself, which was up on a raised platform. The corner of the platform facing the junction functioned as something of a parapet. It reminded me of a castle battlement. From up there, one had a commanding view of the scene. It was also from that location that arrows were shot at the police. One arrow hit an officer in the lower leg. Rocks and petrol bombs were fired from home-made catapults.

After scouting out the situation, I went inside the campus. As at CUHK, I was part of a group ensuring necessary supplies got to the people there. The main supply station was right inside the main entrance. Supplies were streaming in. It didn't seem much was needed at the moment, and that was confirmed by everyone I asked. We're OK, they said. In the midst of the action, with things flying fast and thick, nobody really had much time to think. It was all they could do to gather the supplies that were already streaming in. When I pressed them, they said goggles, raincoats, face scarves, gloves. "What about food?" I asked. They looked at me like they thought I was kidding. "What if you're here for a while?" I added, by way of explanation. People weren't really thinking too much ahead at that point. I put out the call on Telegram and WhatsApp groups, and within an hour people in the supply network were delivering the needed items.

I put in a shift at the scrubbing station, work I was familiar with from previous protests. Water didn't wash off the blue dye or the burning sensation of the toxic chemicals. Only rubbing alcohol did that effectively, and it was in short supply. We only had small alcohol wipes, so it was painstaking work cleaning people. First they would get hosed down and then whatever that didn't wash away had to be scrubbed. Lots of protesters didn't bother; they just rushed right back out to the front line.

Towards evening, the police did start to attack from another direction, the east. They tried to cross the Cheong Wan Road bridge that passed over the Cross-Harbour Tunnel entrance. Now they were coming from two points, the east and the west, on Cheong Wan Road. As the light began to fade, the intensity of the police attacks increased; until then, there had been something almost laconic about them. Now it was as if they suddenly wanted to make a breakthrough before dark.

Well-prepared on the bridge, having set up barricades at the mid-point, protesters started a huge fire that billowed metres into the air. Police appeared surprised at the strength of the resistance. They sent a dark-green Unimog armoured truck over the bridge towards the barricade, as if intent on crashing through it. Protesters rained so many petrol bombs down on the vehicle that it caught fire. The flaming Unimog reversed slowly to the foot of the bridge, where cops put out the fire with hand-held extinguishers.

The police had managed to turn a minor problem into a major crisis. Where that morning there were maybe somewhere between 100 and 200 protesters on campus, the number had now ballooned into the thousands, most, like myself, having arrived after having heard the call for reinforcements.

As early as 4pm, police had warned that they labelled the situation a riot. Anyone who happened to be in the area, whether directly involved or helping in any way, risked being arrested for rioting; all were urged to leave.

From then, the siege descended slowly but surely. By eight o'clock or so, it was difficult for reinforcements to enter PolyU. Police blocked access to Hung Hom MTR station on the east side; even the media were barred. The length of Chatham Road South, bordering the campus to the west and north, was also blocked. And by an hour later, it was difficult if not impossible to find a way into or out of the campus.

Over the hours, I could see this coming and knew that if I wanted to, I could still leave. My partner was away from Hong Kong. My kids were being looked after by a good friend, a protester herself who would understand a protester's priorities. Even before I asked, she offered to look after them through the night. The kids wouldn't be pleased but would accept it; they too knew what the struggle was about.

It had taken more time for the situation to dawn on others, but as it did, it became the constant topic of discussion. What should we do? Should we go or stay? Few made a decision about this. Everyone deferred to everyone else: it's not up to me to decide, it depends on what the majority want. But who was to figure out what that was, especially given the chaos and the fact people were spread out all over the large campus? Others felt that the sacrifices had already been so high, we had to persist. But persist in what exactly, for what exactly?

It wasn't only my children I thought about and how they would be without a parent through the night or even longer. It wasn't only that I thought about what would happen if I were arrested – I would likely be detained for up to 48 hours, which meant the children would go 48 more hours without a parent; I could be brought straight to court and denied bail, indefinitely, until the end of the trial. Based on what the police had already said, I stood a good chance of being charged with riot, which had a maximum sentence of 10 years in prison, over half of their childhood; all that simply because I had decided to stay, not out of conviction but in spite of my ambivalence, or hadn't even quite decided to, but just ended up staying by default. It wasn't only that. I also looked around me at the others, most of whom were young people, yes, significantly older than my young children, but they still brought out the parental instinct in me, and I thought about how they had parents who worried about them but were not there, could not be there. How would they feel about their children being trapped? My children were there, and I was here. Their children were here, and they were there. All of us separated.

And so a decision was made by default, by the others and by myself. And when the cordon closed, that was that; there was no way out. The decision of whether to go or stay had been made for us.

As soon as police sealed the campus, they issued a

statement not dissimilar from the first, a kind of reiteration: "Anyone who enters or stays on the campus and assists rioters in any way will risk committing the offence of taking part in a riot." About an hour later, the police made another announcement. They threatened to enter the campus by force, using lethal means if necessary. All persons present, with the exception of credentialed journalists, would be subject to arrest. They called on protesters to leave the campus via one exit near the Lee Shau Kee Building (Block Y).

It was then that the realisation descended on everyone that we were trapped. And not only were we trapped, but we could be killed by the police storming the campus.

At that point, some, mostly first-aiders and journalists, decided to leave. Their bags were searched and their IDs checked. Four journalists and two first-aiders were seen being arrested at the exit point the police had announced. At least two human-rights observers were also arrested. A day later, police said that they had arrested 51 people who "claimed to be medics or journalists". A widely shared photo showed first-aiders sitting cross-legged on the pavement with their hands tied behind their backs.

Once we heard they were arrested, we knew there was no way out for us. If the police were even going to arrest journalists and first-aiders, what chance did we have? We were well and truly stuck. Protect the Children were a well-known group of mostly older people who often shielded frontline protesters and helped them in other ways. They decided to leave together. The police prevented them from doing so.

After the police cordon was established, they took no additional offensive action. A strange and uneasy calm descended on the campus. Meanwhile, word of the siege got out quickly. Supporters began to gather at the perimeters of the cordon. We heard of thousands of protesters in nearby Tsim Sha Tsui fighting the police, either to divert their attention from PolyU or to make their way to campus. They kept going until deep into the night but weren't able to break through or sufficiently distract the police's attention from us so that we could break out. In fact, the police spent the night fortifying their cordon, and the protester numbers seemed too small. It was, from our point of view, a far too quiet night. Have people given up on us? some wondered. Have they forgotten us?

It is hard to describe the dread of being surrounded like that. There is a special horror that comes with being trapped, in the dark, not knowing what to expect or how long the situation might go on like that, having constantly to be on one's guard, aware that the police could attack at any moment. Especially after the police statement threatening use of lethal force, there was a real fear of loss of life that night (ours, to be precise), a sense the police were capable of anything. Some spoke of the prospect of a massacre and mentioned 4 June.

Some people already had wills or last testaments that they'd written before going on previous protests. Others wrote theirs now. Some circulated them online, along with their particulars. These were not statements bequeathing property to others but last messages, words bequeathed to the world by someone who might cease to exist.

Something in me resisted making my own. Did I not quite believe the situation I was in was real? Was I in denial? My partner said I often failed to realise how serious a situation was until it was too late. Was that the case now? Influenced by the others, I wrote to my family on a small piece of paper:

"If you find this, and I am no longer with you, remember that I love you, and I will always be with you." I dated it, folded it and put it in my wallet. To this day, it's still there.

It didn't take long to see being stuck there would be a huge mental struggle. Someone sobbed hysterically in the dark. Get your fucking shit together, I muttered under my breath. If you keep this up, you're going to fucking lose your mind – and make me lose mine. In a movement, both courage and fear are contagious, and in that compressed situation, even more so. I recognised I had to do my best to control myself. I was angered by others' weakness and fear not because I was without them but precisely because I had them too. But one simply could not to succumb to them, not in a situation like that. This is going to do us in, I said to myself. I had always been of the belief that our own greatest adversary is ourselves. There was howling and shrieking in the darkness. The police could not have done better to unnerve us if they had broadcast on a loop across campus a recording of those eerie human noises. A young man put a pair of scissors to his throat. Friends had to intervene to keep him from cutting himself.

Others were almost preternaturally calm. I heard the following anecdote: Someone pleaded with a man working in the school cafeteria to leave campus together. "No," said the cook. "I'm not leaving as long as others remain. I'm not scared. I'm rioting. Cooking is rioting." I felt that way myself. "Cooking is rioting." The worst for me was the knowledge that just what happened to me was a matter beyond my power alone to decide.

There was also the usual heartening sense of togetherness and thoughtfulness. People went out of their way to look out for each other: Are you hungry? Are you cold? What more could one do in a time of emergency but attend to the animal needs; food, warmth, the things that kept us alive?

Conversation generally avoided the more troubling and existential topics, but at one point deep into the night, I joined a circle of others philosophising about death. One raised the protest slogan 民不畏死奈何死慢之: *If people are not afraid to die, it is of no avail to threaten them with death*, a paraphrase of the *Dao De Jing*. Was it true that we were not afraid to die? Certainly not in my case. The situation made me more aware than ever of all of the things I feared. I thought of the words scrawled on a building not far from where we sat and quoted them aloud: "Give me liberty or give me death."

A girl said, "If it is my time to die, it is my time to die. Of course, I do not wish to die. But I must accept it if this is the way it is to be."

"Today is a good day to die," I said, in English, in such a way as to make clear the words were not my own. I didn't feel I could in that moment express my own thoughts about death, only quote others.

"Old Dog," said another in the circle, also in English.

"Wow," I said. "How did you know that?"

"I've studied the Indians," he said. "They're like us: outnumbered, outgunned, maybe even at risk of annihilation."

"Annihilation?! That's a little exaggerated, isn't it?"

"Not in the sense that the regime wants to do away with any sort of substantial separate Hong Kong identity. The US government never really intended to exterminate all the Indians either, just the ones that got in the way."

"Do you believe that?" the girl asked, motioning to me. "Today is a good day to die?"

"I'm not brave enough to believe it. The Indian warriors

would say that before riding off to battle. I'm too much a coward to ever deliberately bring myself face-to-face with death." I didn't say so, but what was on the tip of my tongue in that moment was, I didn't even intend to be here now.

"Then again," said another, "since no day is a good day to die, I guess every day is as good as any other, today included."

"That's sideways courage," another said.

"Yes, that's the best I can do."

"We all have sideways courage."

"Sideways courage is good. Don't sacrifice yourself needlessly. Save others if you can. Live to fight another day."

The girl pulled her mask down from her face. I could hardly see her face in the dark, but her contours gradually grew into focus. In that moment, it struck me as magnificently human, a face I would always remember, an emblem of humanity. It probably had that effect because we were surrounded by people in masks. Looking at her face, it struck me that it had been a while since I had seen someone's face.

"Put that back on," a voice scolded. "This place is crawling with cops. There could be some among us."

So she did.

There were hundreds of us in all, though because of the size of the campus and the tense situation, it was hard to get a sense of exactly how many. Maybe a couple thousand altogether. We didn't all gather in one place at any one time, and even that first night, many seemed to have gone into hiding or were at least lying low.

There were many types: frontline protesters, first-aiders, the mostly older members of the Protect the Children group who'd tried to leave and were barred, housewives volunteering to cook in the campus canteen, university students, lots of secondary students, a pro-democracy Legco member who'd decided to stay in solidarity with the others and even a few parents who'd come looking for their kids and got stuck there themselves. The police called us all rioters. Not many were PolyU students; a lot of us easily got lost on the large campus, and it was hard to find someone who knew the way.

Our motives and desires were mixed. Some expressed willingness to defend the campus to the death, others had never intended to get stuck there. Some wanted to leave. None expressed regret about being there. Perhaps they didn't want to share that for fear of disheartening others. In spite of the difficulties of the situation, the common protest spirit prevailed: 齊上齊落, *we advance and retreat together*. At least to begin with.

Because of our diversity, because we were spread out all over, because this was a situation none of us ever intended to be in, it was hard to decide collectively on any course of action. Sentries were posted at all the entrances to the campus. There were many discussions about whether to try to break out. There was no mention of surrender, or of giving up, or of turning ourselves in.

Apart from the sentries, almost all organised attempts at defence, not even to mention attack, ceased as soon as we saw we were under siege. Petrol bomb manufacture stopped, though there were still boxes of them that were dispersed to the various entry points. Some got fed up with the lengthy discussions that arrived at no decision, pre-empting them with, Let's break out now. They would then stomp away as if heading towards the front line, as if testing to see whether others would follow, but no escape attempts materialised during the night.

Dozing off, slumped in a chair, I was startled awake by a boom emerging out of the eerie silence of the night, followed by shouting from the direction of the main entrance. I looked at my phone: it was just after five in the morning. I scolded myself, I knew you'd drop your guard and be made to pay, as I ran over to the brick parapet above the entrance. I looked down: it was so dark I could hardly see. I heard shooting and then, as my eyes adjusted, saw two protesters come out of the darkness pursued by the black-clad raptors, who caught and subdued them. Straddled atop them, they were beginning to get out their plastic twist-ties to bind their wrists behind their backs. I couldn't see all of the details, but their actions were so familiar from previous arrests as to be unmistakeable. No one could say they weren't methodical, well-trained.

As soon as the protesters up on the podium saw the raptors down below, they rained petrol bombs down on them. The whole area exploded in flames. They spread everywhere and grew rapidly, engulfing the expanse in fire. The fire was so intense, I wondered whether the entrance had been booby-trapped, flammable liquid poured over the barricades, much of which was made up of wooden furniture scavenged from the university buildings. How else to explain a place made of brick burning so quickly? In that enclosed space, it was the most intense fire I had seen in months of fires being set on the streets, at MTR entrances, in Party-owned banks and pro-Communist shops. Perhaps because I had just woken up, this whole episode had a dream-like, apocalyptic quality: it seemed in those moments as if the world were on fire. Bang. Bang. Bang. Several explosions in rapid succession.

The all-encompassing flames seemed to terrify even the raptors. They retreated, dragging the detained protesters with them. It got so hot we had to step away from the edge, but before long, the flames began to die down: in that brick-clad environment, there was only so much fuel to consume.

Those who'd been there from the start said the police had attacked with water cannon and followed that up with tear gas and rubber bullets. Was it the invasion we'd been bracing for? Had it been repelled? That, at least, was the impression from where we stood. My hunch was the police were probing, and had the attack not met such an emphatic response, they would have tried to storm the campus.

It was after that I decided to leave. I'd already been considering trying to escape in the morning. I'd spent the night away from my children, who'd been kindly looked after by someone who wasn't their parent. I hadn't been able to contact my partner, abroad, who wouldn't be happy at my decision to stay, to leave the kids in someone else's care for the whole night. There wasn't much else I could do on the campus besides provide moral support. If I wasn't a parent, I think I would have stayed. The somebody else's children would have to fend for themselves; I had my own to get back to. Not exactly the warrior mentality the revolution needed, but so be it.

I didn't tell anyone of my decision, but I got the Telegram contacts of those I trusted. Surely some could surmise what I was up to, though it wasn't uncommon to hook up on Telegram just so people could communicate from one end of the campus to the other. If they guessed, they did not ask, and I did not tell. I feared it would dishearten them to let them know, or lessen my chances of escape, and I wanted to leave alone. It was the way of getting out that stood the best chance of success. Plus, I was ashamed of my selfishness.

Not long after it got light, dressed in non-black civilian

clothes, I put into action a plan that had been in the back of my mind ever since the prospect of getting trapped on campus arose. I'd noticed when I first arrived on the PolyU campus that Monday, now exactly a week ago, when the main entrance was first barricaded after the first police tear gas attack, that not too far from that entrance was a building that had a small door that opened onto the street. The campus is built on a platform, or podium, as it is usually called, but most of the buildings have levels that descend below the platform to street level. I went down through that building and found the single door. I opened it and walked out into the morning.

I'd scouted out the police positions from the podium just beforehand, so I had some sense of the areas to avoid, at least among those that were immediately visible from campus. I kept down low and managed to make my way across Cheong Wan Road. But that wasn't really the area I was most concerned about; it was the outer edge of the cordon that couldn't be seen from the campus. I found a long hedge of bushes and hid behind it.

From there, I could see clumps of police in riot gear stationed at various spots. The cordon enveloped some areas in East Tsim Sha Tsui that included buildings that housed shops and residences. People were exiting these buildings and passing through the police cordon as well as passing through the cordon in the other direction to get to them. My best bet was to get to those buildings and then proceed as if I was exiting them myself. On my phone, I checked an address and memorised it in case the police quizzed me. When one group of police were checking IDs at the outer edge of the cordon and another was looking away, I crawled out of the hedge and walked as quickly as I could to the nearest building. From there, I walked to the cordon's edge, where I was stopped. I pointed to the building I'd just come out of, and the police motioned me through without demanding further details. It could not have been easier. It paid not to be young, to able to "not look like a protester".

After managing to get out, my first feeling was relief. Followed immediately by guilt. It was the latter that lingered long after the former had passed. Guilt at having abandoned the others, guilt at leaving them to their fate. Were we not all in this together? Did we not "advance and retreat together"? Apparently not any more. Apparently not me.

No possible justification satisfied my conscience, but the one that came closest to placating it was the defence that now I was outside, I could help those inside in other ways. That was partly true but wasn't really the reason I left. The reason I left was I wanted to see my kids. Or, more precisely, the idea of my kids being elsewhere left me feeling that I was in the wrong place.

It turned out that I had chosen the most opportune moment to leave. Not long after I got out, police in East Tsim Sha Tsui started pushing the cordon outward, forcing the hundreds gathered a good distance from them, obviously there out of concern for those at PolyU, to back away a couple hundred metres. What could have caused the police to act like that? I wondered.

It didn't take long to find out: About a hundred protesters had tried to escape together. They just went straight down the steps of the main entrance out onto the road. They figured there was strength in numbers and sneaking away would be futile. They were attacked by massive amounts of tear gas and rubber bullets. Most retreated to the campus, a few were arrested.

I walked back through East Tsim Sha Tsui and began to have another premonition of entrapment, especially when I saw the police extending their cordon from PolyU down along Chatham Road. At that point, all I wanted was to get away. I circumvented the end of the cordon and passed into Tsim Sha Tsui proper.

Not long after that, police swooped and arrested about a hundred in East Tsim Sha Tsui. All of the protesters I'd seen there had been peaceful, and were doing no more than milling about, but the police were apparently afraid there was some plot afoot to aid an escape. So many were arrested, two hired coaches were brought in to take them away.

I contacted people on campus. *How are you doing?*

Everyone's afraid, came the reply. *And tired. They say food's going to run out soon. There's not enough drinking water.* Some said, *We're just trying to figure out how to get out*.

Others, *We're planning to stay, we have no intention of leaving*.

I told them how I got out.

That way's blocked now, they said. *Lots of police right across the road from there*. The thwarted escape attempt had alerted police and made it even more difficult to find a way out.

Meanwhile, online appeals had gone out to go on strike that day, a Monday, and go to Tsim Sha Tsui to help free those under siege at PolyU.

Crossing Chatham Road South into Tsim Sha Tsui was like passing from one world to another: the streets were so full of protesters, I had to stay. It was such a joy to be "back among my own", and the prospect of perhaps being able to do something to help the people inside tantalised. This was the first time I planned to go home but didn't.

Along the streets perpendicular to Chatham Road, barricades were being constructed with bamboo poles gathered from a nearby building site. An actual bamboo scaffolder was directing the operation.

But even before the barricades could be completed, police charged, pushing us back onto Nathan Road, the main thoroughfare of Tsim Sha Tsui which ran all down the spine of central Kowloon.

That's how the morning and much of the rest of the day played out: we got pushed farther and farther away from our goal, PolyU, northward up Nathan Road, first past Jordan Road, and then, after a pause, past Gascoigne Road, and then nearly up to Waterloo Road. We were supposed to be trying to get to PolyU but spent most of the day going in the opposite direction, under almost constant tear gas barrage. Every time a barricade was built, we were pushed back again and had to abandon it.

Two other escape attempts were made from PolyU in the early afternoon. Just as had happened in the morning when the first occurred, police pushed the protesters outside the cordon farther away. More and more protesters were arriving, but police were entrenched and determined to hold their lines. Protesters made a concerted effort to push through on both Gascoigne and Jordan Roads, without success.

On Gascoigne Road in particular, there was a constant barrage of tear gas. It got so thick that I ducked into a side street to get a breath of semi-fresh air. There I saw a nun in her white habit, looking very prim, tidy and clean, almost a mirage. She was probably in her seventies, impossibly petite: she had grown up in a time when nutrition was not what it is today. A young assistant tried to hold her by the elbow, but she clearly had a mind of her own; she was guiding him, not the reverse. She was making her way ever so slowly up the street towards Gascoigne Road, apparently because she was curious about what was happening and wanted to have a look.

"Sister, be careful!" I said. "It's dangerous up there."

She acknowledged me, nodding in my direction, and continued.

Suddenly, a half dozen cops poked their heads above the railing of the West Kowloon Corridor, the flyover road directly above Gascoigne, and looked straight down at us. It was as if the devil had descended out of the heavens.

I pointed at the nun and shouted up to them, "Be careful to avoid her, she's not a part of this!"

From behind me, a voice said, "What are you, stupid? They're not going to listen to you."

My plea confused the cops for just a moment. They looked back and forth between me, on one side of the street, and the nun on the other. Then one raised his rifle and fired directly at the nun.

Police should never aim tear gas right at someone. Around the world, there were many cases of people dying from getting hit by tear gas canisters. Human Rights Watch had recently documented the deaths of at least 16 protesters killed by tear gas cartridges in Iraq.

All through the confrontation, the cops up on the flyover had been creeping along and intermittently ducking up to shoot not only directly at people but right down at their heads. Misuse of tear gas had been a constant issue throughout the protests, with police also shooting it at people who were trapped in areas where they couldn't disperse and even inside of MTR stations.

The nun was standing next to a high compound wall surrounding a school (a Catholic school; I imagined that was where she'd come from). The canister hit the wall a foot or two from her head and ricocheted, skittering off further down the street.

As I watched, the same cop turned his rifle towards me and took aim. Someone behind me, probably the same one who told me how stupid I was to bother appealing to the cops, yanked my arm from behind, pulling me into another side street perpendicular to the nun's.

I turned to see the tear gas canister aimed at me bounce off the building that had been behind me and land not far from the nun, who was still standing in the same place.

"Run!" I yelled, as if she could. The young assistant was trying to tug her backward. I wanted to help her get to safety but was myself pulled down the street back towards Nathan Road.

By late afternoon, I had become exhausted from choking on tear gas all day and lack of sleep. Except for the few moments dozing off before the police invasion that morning, I'd had none in nearly 36 hours.

Our protests had never been designed to fight this sort of more traditional battle having to do with holding or taking territory. We were trying to do what we were least equipped to do. I was frustrated and thought if I stayed any longer, I risked becoming a danger to myself and others. It was time to go.

I heard people had started gathering again in East Tsim Sha Tsui after the police swoop in the morning; among them were the parents of those trapped inside. I had to show solidarity. This was the second time I planned to go home but didn't.

I found the parents, dozens of them, sitting on the pavement as close to the police cordon as they could get. Their children were only a few hundred metres away, but the gap between them was so unbridgeable as to seem immense. Their heads were bowed. They held handmade cardboard placards in front of their chests: "Set our kids free!"

I couldn't bear to ask them anything about themselves or their kids, so I just sat there with them to show support and said useless things like, I'm sure your kid's OK. Don't worry, s/he'll come out safely.

Stand News, the plucky little upstart pro-democracy media organisation that somehow managed to be everywhere and cover everything with a fraction of the mainstream media's resources, did dare to ask them what messages they wanted to send their children and the world.

The mother of a secondary student said, "My beloved son, be good and do not lose hope…take good care of yourself and look after the other kids… My greatest hope is you will come home safe and sound, that you will come back unscathed."

The mother of two daughters who were university students said, "I cannot stop you from standing up for a just cause. I love you, and I am proud of you… I do not want to become Chan Yin-lam's mother. I do not want to become the Tiananmen Mothers." (Chan Yin-lam was a 15-year-old who mysteriously disappeared and was found dead in the harbour two months earlier.)

Parents of a 19-year-old volunteer first-aider said, "We are behind you. Please look after yourself when you help other kids… Many people are supporting you. Do not ever lose faith. Faith matters! Remember that!"

Listening to the parents, I was reminded that the protests

were not only a youth rebellion but involved all of society, not only as participants but because these young people had parents, teachers, friends. Many older people felt guilty that it was the young people having to sacrifice because they in their time had not themselves done enough for the freedom struggle. The uprising was a society-wide web of such deep relationships. That was why it couldn't be defeated by force. Of course, the police could inflict upon those at PolyU however much suffering they wished, but they couldn't vanquish them because most of the people who identified with them, supported them, had fought beside them and loved them were on the outside.

At around eight that evening, nearly 100 performed a daring escape from the campus by lowering themselves down ropes from a bridge onto a road between the main campus and a satellite. The bridge was on the far side of the campus from the main entrance. People had noticed there were few to no police guarding it. On the other side of the bridge, police waited, so there was no way to get out by crossing the bridge.

Instead, an intricate escape was planned that involved not only the people inside lowering themselves the seven or eight metres from the bridge to the ground but also people on motorbikes coming to fetch them and speed them away. All of this was undertaken with astounding precision and rapidity within the space of less than a half hour. Police caught on fast to what was happening and rushed to the scene, later announcing they'd made 37 arrests. Even though many dozens got out, the feat was far from entirely successful.

Tens of thousands of others attempted to make it through from the outside world to PolyU until deep into the night. None succeeded. The police went on the offensive. They cornered and arrested people by the hundreds. That 24-hour period would turn out to have the most arrests by far of any in the protests – more than 1,000 in all. More than 200 arrested in a single location on Nathan Road would eventually go on trial for riot, the biggest single trial in Hong Kong history, so big that it was spread out among five courthouses around the city.

Towards midnight, about 35 hours after I'd last been there, I decided to go home. This time I actually did.

The kids were already in bed, having gone to sleep hours before for the second night in a row without me. I crept in to watch them sleep. I bent down and kissed my young daughter, the eldest, good night. Half-opening her eyes, she groggily asked, "Baba, where were you?"

"Oh, just at the protests."

"OK," she said, and went back to sleep.

*

Early the next day, I went back, and no one was there.

People had given up. There would be no more large-scale attempts to break people out of PolyU.

But the siege would go on, for many days yet, 12 in all. And so would the escape attempts.

The news from inside was not good. People were becoming more distraught, more distrustful of one another and everyone else, more desperate to get out. There was a fear of undercover police in their midst, coupled with the constant fear that police would soon attack. Those remaining kept their distance from one another, avoided eye contact. Some appeared disoriented, mentally decomposing.

In the first few days, various prominent figures, from a

retired pro-Communist politician to a group of secondary school principals to the pro-democracy Legco representatives for the education and medical functional constituencies, managed to procure the release of, in all, hundreds trapped inside, mostly secondary students and volunteer first-aiders. Others were medically evacuated. The terms of the agreements between the prominent personages and the police were that those who exited under their guidance would not be immediately arrested but would all be searched and have their details taken. Police reserved the right to arrest them at a later date.

Among protesters both inside PolyU and outside, there was much debate as to whether these releases constituted surrender, whether they were honourable, whether they constituted abandonment of those who remained inside. But at the same time, one couldn't really blame a teenager who wanted no more than to go home, a volunteer first-aider who'd come to provide emergency medical treatment to others and ended up trapped inside, any more than a father who had to go home to look after his kids could be blamed. None of us were heroes, and all of us were. Or perhaps, all of us were heroes, and none of us were.

At any rate, their departure left the numbers remaining inside seriously depleted, down to the hundreds.

A network quickly arose to help those remaining inside escape. The code for the helpers was "parents", for those inside, "children".

On the day I left, dozens of others escaped as well, alone or in small groups; the largest number at one time was five. These escapes were largely unaided.

The next day, at least 14 made their way out through the sewage tunnels. That was the beginning of a massive operation. Sewer maps were sent via Telegram to those inside. Engineers and those familiar with the sewage system helped, keeping track of water levels, calculating the best times for escape attempts. Others would work their way back through the tunnels from the outside towards the campus to check if routes were clear. Others still would wait with cars near the manhole covers on the outside, so that when the escapees emerged above ground, they would be immediately whisked away. In all, an estimated 200 escaped via the sewage tunnels.

The media reported on others who escaped. I myself knew of 22 whose escapes had never made it into the press. Together with the 100 or so who abseiled down the ropes from the bridge on the 18th and the 200 who came through the tunnels, somewhere between 300 and 400 escaped, dropping from a bridge, hands torn open from the ropes; crawling through sewers, covered in shit; running for their lives across the roads and through the bushes.

The police caught many others, a dozen here and a dozen there, day after day, especially during the first few days. In all, some 1,100 were arrested leaving PolyU; in addition, about 300 minors had their ID details taken, with the prospect of future arrest always hanging over them. Among the arrested "rioters" were 59 from the Protect the Children group, the 51 first-aiders arrested on the first night of the siege when the police demanded that all leave the campus, plus dozens of other first-aiders and social workers who left in subsequent days.

*

During all that time, as the gruelling saga of the police siege of PolyU played itself out before the eyes of Hong Kong people, the streets remained mostly quiet if tense. It was hard to know why, but rather than dejection at the failure to break the siege, most thought it had to do with upcoming District Council elections. (District Councils were the lowest rung of the governmental ladder, essentially powerless and advisory in their function, and therefore also the only bodies in Hong Kong whose representatives were elected almost entirely according to principles of genuine universal suffrage.) There were rumours that the regime was looking for an excuse to postpone or even cancel the elections, and there was no better excuse than "violence". With few to no protests, the regime had no excuse, and the elections were held on the 24th, as scheduled, while the siege was still going on, exactly one week after it began.

They resulted in a landslide victory for pro-democracy candidates, who won 392 of the 452 seats, or 86 per cent. The vote was a de facto referendum on the protests, on the government and the police, on the siege of PolyU; it was unequivocally clear where the vast majority of Hong Kong stood. In several District Councils, pro-democracy candidates won 100 per cent of the seats, including in places like Wong Tai Sin and Tai Po that were hardly traditional pro-democracy bastions but had experienced some of the heaviest tear gas attacks. Police attacks on protesters and citizens throughout the city had turned the city against the police and their masters.

The election results emphatically reinforced the consistent findings of countless opinion polls over the months, but the government had up to then continued to use the propaganda line that the "silent majority" of Hong Kong people supported the government and opposed "violence" (that is, the protests). The elections showed that the reason that majority was so silent was that it didn't exist.

The day after their victory, the first thing that the hundreds of newly elected pro-democracy district councillors did was to go to PolyU, accompanied by hundreds of other protesters, to demand that police end the siege.

But not until the 29th, 12 days after it had first begun, would the siege eventually be lifted. Police entered the campus the day before, the 28th.

This was after a two-day search by PolyU management that had turned up a single, solitary protester, a woman sleeping on a couch who appeared disoriented, mentally unstable. PolyU counsellors encouraged her to leave, but she didn't listen to them and went wandering off to a place nobody knew, never to be seen again.

Another protester, Ah Bong, spoke to the press the night before police were to enter the campus. Two others spoke in a Facebook Live video. So there were still a few around. But almost all surrenders and apprehensions occurred in the days after the beginning of the siege.

When the police entered, only a few did so initially. By a few hours later, though, the campus was swarming with hundreds of them "collecting evidence". Police seemed particularly intent on demonstrating to the media their finds of combustible liquids, to show how dangerous the rioters were, just what they were up against.

Not a single protester was found.

The police were doing their best to look purposeful, to show they were on a righteous mission, but by then, police appeared as desperate for the siege to end as anyone else. It all appeared so senseless and futile. The police had scored another massive own goal. Our indomitable spirit had prevailed. Or so it seemed at the time.

*

The District Council election victory wasn't the only significant event that occurred during the siege, which lasted from the 17th to the 29th. The Hong Kong Human Rights and Democracy Act and PROTECT Hong Kong Act were passed by the US Senate on 19 November, passed by the House on the 20th, almost unanimously by both, and signed into law by the president on the 27th, two days before the end of the siege, which had given passage of the bill an added urgency.

District Council elections and the passage of the two acts in the US seemed a culmination after months of protests, accomplishments in their own right, though far from any sort of final victory. In themselves, they brought us no closer to our positive objectives, the fulfilment of the five demands, including genuine universal suffrage. We had to fight so hard to achieve so little; still, they were something, a kind of vindication. The Hong Kong people and the world's most powerful democracy were on our side. But we couldn't relax for long; the struggle had to go on.

The other apparent outcome of the siege was harder for me to come to terms with. Frontliners stopped coming out, not entirely but on any kind of large scale. It had been expected that they would go silent around the time of the District Council elections, to deny the government the excuse of "violence" as a pretext for postponing or even calling off elections that everyone expected the pro-democracy movement to win big. And at first, I thought, Well, they need a rest.

But then disruptive actions were called the week following the end of the PolyU siege. These calls had always been hit and miss; sometimes they happened, sometimes not. This time they didn't.

What was up? There had been a debate on LIHKG, the most popular online forum for young frontline protesters, and a significant number thought it wasn't wise to go out: the actions had been so well publicised so long in advance that they gave the police far too much time to prepare and took the advantage away from protesters.

Fair enough, but even after that, they didn't come. And didn't come. Until more than a month had passed. Never before had the frontline protesters gone so long without taking major action.

In the meantime, we held mass marches, one of 380,000 on 1 December and another a week later of 800,000. Frontline protesters were present at those in large numbers but decided against taking any spin-off actions of their own, not least at the request of protest organisers and also because police were again prepared to crack down hard and could do so well enough considering they were concentrated in the areas where the marches occurred.

At first, I thought the frontliner stand-down was just momentary. Then it began to dawn on me that maybe they wouldn't come out again. Had the PolyU siege affected their morale more than I had realised? I remembered how surprised I was four years earlier at how depressed people were after the Umbrella Movement. Was it like that now? How thick was I? How much of nothing did I not understand? as one of my frontline friends always asked me.

I asked again: What's up?

Different people said different things. So many comrades

had been lost. They could do nothing against the police. They needed to escalate but didn't have the weapons.

None of this sounded convincing. Nothing's changed, I responded. Don't you remember that the actions you took the week between Chow Tsz-lok's death and the PolyU siege were among the most successful of the protests? They brought the transport system to all but a halt and closed down many institutions and events. So now you're telling me that the conclusion you draw from the PolyU siege and the failure to break it is that disruptive actions are in vain? Have you suddenly lost heart, after all these months of saying, "Give me liberty or give me death"?

It wasn't my place to tell people who risked so much what to do, but my discussions with them made me see the extent to which the struggle was psychological: it existed within us; it had to do with the stories we told ourselves, and how we told them.

The success of the movement had come from the combination of non-violent and more aggressive, disruptive protests. Where would we be without the latter? The frontline protesters had given the movement momentum. They drove it, kept it on the front foot, the government and police on the back foot, often wrong-footing them. They provided a focal point, a rallying point. They were deeply important symbolically – iconic. It was up to us oldsters to stand up for the youngsters, but if the youngsters weren't there, what were we oldsters to do? We could still come out to march in our hundreds of thousands, but as we had seen time and time again, the government had perfected the art of ignoring that.

The government had repeatedly said it would do nothing until there was "peace". Well, by late December, there had been over a month of relative peace since the PolyU siege, and the government had continued to do nothing. One effect of the absence of large-scale frontline protests was to call its bluff: it was obviously going to do nothing whether there was "violence" or not. Doing nothing was its default mode. It had done nothing and would do nothing, peace or violence.

I drew different conclusions from the PolyU siege. It showed that nothing the government and police did could break us, as long as we didn't break ourselves. Every victory of theirs was pyrrhic. They were backed into a corner and as long as they tried to settle the conflict and the political crisis solely through force, intimidation and propaganda, they were destined to lose, again and again. As ever, as long as there was resistance, there was hope. Victory lay in our hands, years down the road perhaps, but it was ours for the taking.

Not everyone was persuaded by this line of reasoning, to be sure. And I wondered, after months of worrying almost every weekend, whether this would be our last. Such a thought was alarmist and premature: after all, once again in December, millions had marched, as they had in all previous months. The revolution rolled on. But without the frontliners, it was different, perhaps becoming something else.

Others said an extended break might not be such a bad thing. And even if frontliners stopped coming out in large numbers, that hardly meant the movement was over. Changed, yes, significantly, and exactly how one couldn't foresee, but substantially, certainly. But the movement was more than that. It consisted of at least three prongs: the protests; community work, grass-roots democratisation and working within the electoral system such as it was (rigged, only partially democratic), including the 2020 Legco elections; and international lobbying. If you took frontline protests away from that equation, the equation changed, no doubt about it, but by how much and how exactly, no one could say.

Over Christmas, disruptive but smaller actions took place, mostly in the vicinity of malls, and police ramped up arrests again – 370 in the Christmas week alone. But as the year changed, the ongoing absence of large-scale frontline protests added an element of uncertainty to the outlook of the movement. Most shrugged and didn't seem to think this was as much of a problem as I was making it out to be. Maybe I was just too nervous; maybe after all this time I still hadn't learned that the movement would somehow, some way take care of itself.

BLACK ANGELS

攬炒

If we burn, you burn with us

*– protest slogan borrowed from
The Hunger Games: Mockingjay*

"What's that?"

Shouts and screams came from main street.

We were just about to go to bed, a little before midnight on a relatively quiet evening before the big day to come. The first of October, the PRC national day. Major protests were called to mark the "day of mourning". Before going to bed, I'd packed my backpack, each item chosen carefully: as ever, there was the prospect that, rather than coming home, I might end up in jail instead.

"Hit him! Beat him!" A woman's shrill voice. Then the roar of an attack and screams.

The neighbourhood's topography was bowl-like, creating a peculiar acoustic effect: from where we lived, we could hear most everything on main street and the concrete football pitch beyond, the outdoor karaoke, the cheers when a goal was scored.

"I had better go see what's happening," I said, putting my clothes back on and heading out.

The main street was a couple hundred metres away. As soon as I turned the corner, I was enveloped by a swirl of dozens of faces and bodies. I'd lived in the neighbourhood for years, knew all the types, could classify them at first glance, yet it was still hard to orient myself. It was like walking into a dream, or nightmare.

A couple dozen thugs stood around two large round tables outside a bar. Many prowled the street, threatening anyone who came near. They glared, fists raised; several lunged, drunk, rageful, looking for blood.

Across the way I saw two young men in front of the local government office. It took but a glance to see they had been viciously beaten. Their faces were bruised, swollen and full of cuts. It hurt just to look at them. They were conscious but looked dazed. A tall woman stood in front of them, legs spread wide, blocking anyone who might have the idea of inflicting more damage. Others gathered near her, also attempting to draw a protective cordon around the victims, while the thugs, just a few metres away, taunted them. At another bar open to the street, patrons had withdrawn inside, shocked and cowering.

"Has anyone called 999?" I said. A few said yes. I asked the group gathered near the beaten men what had happened.

People seemed too shaken to put together a clear, coherent account, but it wasn't hard to gather the gist: the young men had been attacked by the thugs. I shouted, "This is an emergency situation. Let's wait until the ambulance and police arrive. Everyone should stay here until then." Even as those words came out of my mouth, a voice in my head said, Who am I kidding? I had no faith in the police.

One of the thugs, a bit older, about my age, gave me a hard shove. "Get out of here! Go home!" he shouted in my face.

Behind him, the same woman I'd heard shrilly shouting from my home egged him on: "Get him! Beat him!"

I raised my arms in the air: I had no interest in fighting.

She mocked, "Oh, so you're one of those protesters? You think you're better than us. We'll show you! Hit him! Beat him!"

Another woman I took to be the man's wife tugged at his shirt and pleaded with him to stop, probably fearing he was getting himself into trouble.

He shoved me up against a stack of old plastic milk crates in front of a grocery. They tumbled over. I took off my glasses and held them in my hand. That was the one clear thought in my mind: I just don't want him to break my glasses; they're the only pair I own.

He shoved me up against the metal shutters of another shop (it was late – except for the bars, all the businesses were closed). He shoved me to the ground and made to punch me. On my back, I put my feet up to block him. Others helped the woman I thought was his wife to pull him away.

While I was being shoved about, an ambulance arrived. The paramedics were attending to the two who'd been beaten. The thugs had used the assault on me as a screen to smuggle the ones whom witnesses had identified as the worst culprits away from the scene. A stocky, muscular guy with dyed blonde hair in a sky-blue T-shirt, who'd been stomping around like a bull, was being led away.

Who are these people? I wondered. In our neighbourhood, if you didn't know everybody, you at least recognised faces, you knew who came from there and who didn't. Among the assailants were some locals, including shopkeepers, but also faces I'd never seen before.

Fifteen long minutes after I got there, the police showed up, all two of them. Their station was about the same distance from the scene as my home. The ambulance, stationed farther away, beat them there by a good five minutes.

It wasn't as if the cops had much else to do: our neighbourhood was regarded as a sleepy place where nothing ever happened. The cops there were the sorts the force didn't want anywhere else, the rejects, the ones being put out to pasture. Through all the months of protests, there hadn't been a single protest in our neighbourhood, nor any altercation between police and protesters. The only sign of the movement was a small Lennon Wall that the local thugs had torn down repeatedly, punching out a man for posting something there.

It was a "blue" neighbourhood, one of the bluest in the city. The power structure was clan-based. The clan leaders maintained a cooperative relationship with the police and were the de facto local authorities. There had always been an air of lawlessness about it. The rule of law that supposedly obtained in the rest of the city didn't quite reach there; the police were hands off. The clan leaders were also the landlords and construction bosses. The clans themselves were strictly hierarchical. Outsiders, which meant anyone from elsewhere in the city, were tolerated as long as they brought their money, paid their rent, patronised the shops, kept their mouths shut. There was peace as long as everyone stayed in their place.

Before long, several more officers arrived. I pointed out to them the people who'd told me they'd witnessed the assaults as well as the few people they'd indicated had been the main culprits who were still present. The officers looked through me. I repeated myself. They nodded but ignored me. I said, "If you don't deal with the matter now, people will lose confidence in you." I left out the fact that they already had, across the city. Distrust was the norm. Four months into the protests, police were regarded as the oppressor; you didn't go to them for help, you tried your best to avoid them.

It didn't take long after the police got there for everyone – assailants, victims, witnesses, bystanders – to realise they weren't going to do anything. That was another dream-like moment: a chill descended. The police took no statements and talked to no one who'd witnessed the attacks. The witnesses and bystanders evaporated. The thugs remained, emboldened.

They threatened me right in front of the officers. "Look," I said. "Look what they're doing right in front of you." The police told me to leave, ironically just as the thugs had done. They apparently faulted me for exacerbating the situation. I looked around and saw I was one of the few non-thugs, non-police left. Some of the officers were talking to the thugs. They seemed to be commiserating with them, nodding their heads sympathetically. Though the police urged me to leave, there was no safe way to get out of there. The thugs had the area surrounded.

The scene was a spooky echo of one of the most infamous

nights since the protests started: 21 July in Yuen Long, simply referred to as "721". On that night, more than a hundred thugs dressed in white T-shirts attacked people in that corner of the city, way north, near the border with the PRC, a place with a rough reputation, infested by triads. The thugs eventually converged on the MTR station, descending to the platform and even entering the trains, beating people as they went. It took the police nearly an hour to respond.

Police later explained there were protests elsewhere that evening. They were busy at those. But a couple of officers had been seen at the MTR station and then disappeared, and police never seemed otherwise to have difficulty attacking different protests in different parts of the city at the same time. When police finally did arrive, they were seen chatting with the men in white T-shirts who held metal bars and rattan sticks, in much the same way that the cops and the thugs stood side by side conferring just then in front of me.

No one was arrested that night of 21 July. Police were accused of colluding with thugs to attack citizens. The thugs had reportedly been on the lookout for protesters, but almost all of those attacked had no relation to the protests, so indiscriminate were the assaults. When a top government official later said he was saddened by the incident and would even apologise, the government having to accept responsibility, he was berated by police unions and then backtracked: of course, he stood completely by the police. This showed just who had the real power in the city: the line increasingly ran straight from the Party to the police, circumventing the government officials, who appeared superfluous, clueless.

Eventually, over a matter of weeks, 37 suspected assailants were arrested, almost all for unlawful assembly, and seven were prosecuted, but this hardly seemed sufficient for an incident that left 45 people hospitalised. A police superintendent later blamed protesters for the attacks, claiming they had gone there looking for trouble, thus drawing the thugs. Such a clearly counterfactual statement decreased confidence even further, if that were possible, in police impartiality as well as their ability and willingness to investigate properly. A pro-Communist Legco member who'd been seen shaking hands with the white-clad thugs right before the attacks faced no investigation. Pro-Communists had taken to claiming that Lam Cheuk-ting was the person responsible for the clashes. He was a pro-democracy Legco member who got there before the police. He tried to protect people and was beaten himself. Regime allies not only took no responsibility for the attacks but attempted to rewrite the history. The message of the incident and its aftermath to citizens was clear: you are on your own; the people are the enemy we stand united against.

Just as I was wondering how, surrounded by threatening thugs and indifferent police, I was going to get out of there, the black angels arrived. They strode through the crowd. They surrounded me in a protective circle and extracted me. Before long, we'd moved a block away, stopping at the corner I'd turned when I first arrived.

Six middle-aged women, all dressed in black: Ming, who was about to announce her candidacy for District Council; no-nonsense Oiwan, always the one to get things done, among the most effective, reliable people I'd ever met; Kay, a law expert who was frail, slight and walked with crutches due to a childhood illness; deep-voiced Nora; and feisty Yuen-ting, whom I knew much less well; and the pro-democracy restaurant owner's wife whose name I could never remember, looking stately, dignified, statuesque in a long, flowing black dress. Fantastically, phenomenally tough, they'd descended and rescued me. Both the thugs and the police were taken aback and stepped aside.

They were soon joined by even more: "What happened? What can I do to help?" All women, all middle-aged, all dressed in black, all in the neighbourhood pro-democracy WhatsApp group where, I discovered later, the word had gone out.

I stood there at a distance from the thugs but still within view. I wanted them to see this. I knew there was a high chance they would try to come after me when the time was right, when I least expected it, but if there was one thing bullies understood, it was power. And the message was clear: I had protection; if they fooled with me, there would be consequences.

*

The group had coalesced in July, about a month after the protests began. Several dozen were in it; some I'd known for ages and worked with, some a short time, some not at all. It had been a pleasure to discover new allies in the place where I lived: You too! And you! And you! We were careful about enlarging the group too much, for fear of infiltration. To join, you had to be vouched for by a trusted member, hardly a spy-proof method, but a balance had to be struck between vigilance and inclusion.

Most were fairly moderate and middle-aged; I felt like a radical among them. Whenever I wanted to get a sense of what the average pro-democracy person thought about this or that occurrence, this or that idea, I asked them. When the media speculated that more aggressive protest actions would lead to a loss of support among ordinary people, I just checked with the group to confirm my hunch. I was confident their views were widely shared across the city, and invariably they were.

The group was dominated by high-powered women who either had never had children or their children were now grown or they were divorced. Most had solid if uninspiring jobs and earned well. They were unencumbered, with the time to dedicate to the freedom struggle. For some, it was the fight they'd been waiting for all their lives. They were the invisible force of the protests. Young frontline protesters got the lion's share of the media coverage, but they were the fish, this was the water.

There were similar groups across the city, like tiny cells, each self-organised and contributing according to their skills and resources. Throughout, they'd stood firmly by the frontliners, the movement's glue of solidarity. While the frontliners took the fight to the regime, it was people like the ones in my WhatsApp group who gave me confidence that the freedom struggle would be able to sustain itself in the long term.

Their quiet, steady courage and commitment were a constant inspiration. They donated money and supplies, often at a moment's notice. A call would go out: protesters need such-and-such supplies at such-and-such place, and group members would rush off to get them and bring them there immediately. They provided shelter to young protesters kicked out of their homes by their parents and to those hiding from the police. They mobilised everyone in the neighbourhood of even the slightest pro-democracy inclination to attend every large protest.

And now, after months of discussions and preliminary actions, the group was about to field a candidate in the upcoming local District Council elections, no small matter in our "blue" neighbourhood where the representative had always been pro-Communist.

I'd predicted that as District Council elections drew near and word got out that there'd be a viable pro-democracy candidate, the pro-Communists who dominated the neighbourhood would feel threatened and violence could increase. And there it was, on display that evening, though the immediate trigger was not the upcoming elections but something entirely different.

✻

Every year as the PRC national day approached, the pro-Communist powers that be in the neighbourhood organised the hanging of commemorative flags and a billboard-size banner. Often they would do this weeks in advance of the actual 1 October anniversary. I found it oppressive, a symbol of the regime's occupation of Hong Kong and a sign of its attempts to insinuate itself into daily life at the grass-roots level, but year after year I endured it in silence.

Showing some awareness that this year might be more sensitive than usual, they waited until closer to the date, and the banner was smaller, showing a scene from the neighbourhood accompanied by a congratulatory message rather than, as in past years, Tiananmen Gate. It was also hung higher, several metres off the ground, to make it harder to tear down. The flags were multicoloured, long and narrow, the flagpoles bamboo. There were dozens of them and they were placed on railings separating pavement from road all along the main street.

On the night of 29 to 30 September, every single flag on the main street was torn down, the bamboo poles broken in half. On the banner, "Liberate Hong Kong", the most popular protest slogan, was spray-painted in black.

Messages in the WhatsApp group alerted me early the next morning. My first reaction: wonderful! I've been wanting to do that for years; now someone finally has. It didn't take long for people, even some in the group, to suspect me. Several asked if I'd done it. No, I said, but I wish I had.

A member of the group who had a good rapport with the pro-Communist neighbourhood pooh-bahs said their initial reaction was just to let it be; they didn't think it was worth the risk of increasing tensions by putting the flags back up.

But in the late afternoon, a large crew put the flags back up.

Later I heard the orders had come from the top, overruling whatever the neighbourhood powers that be thought best: every neighbourhood in the city had to be festooned, no matter what it took. The Hong Kong government had been so terrified at the prospect of protests on the 1st disrupting the official morning flag-raising ceremony that it decided all officials and guests would remain inside watching it through large glass panes and on TV monitors while hundreds of police guarded the flagpole, setting up a cordon hundreds of metres in radius. But it didn't matter to what lengths they had to go, the Communists demanded their Potemkin village.

Not only did the flags go back up, but for the first time ever, PRC flags were also erected, four large ones on extra-high bamboo poles, as if out of revenge: we'll show you who runs this place!

Or a dare: there had in recent months been many incidents

of PRC flags being torn down, stomped on, burned, thrown into the sea. The "desecration" of the flags had enraged the regime. Regime allies had taken out ads offering rewards for tips leading to the arrest and prosecution of the offenders. While the police had made next to no progress investigating the Yuen Long attacks, they were aggressively rounding up flag-desecration suspects.

As the crew put up the flags, several police officers stood by, as if they were the security detail. It's not hard to see how things stand here, I thought as I passed, my young child on my shoulders. When I got to the end of the long row of flags, I shouted, "Liberate Hong Kong!" The boy on my shoulders reached down and put his hand over my mouth, trying to muzzle it. Funny, I thought, how far down the years fear is felt; even before understanding comes fear. Or was it instinctual prudence?

"I'll liberate you from something!" came a shout back. I didn't look over my shoulder.

That night, the assaults occurred. Because a lot of people had seen or heard I was there that evening (and also heard erroneously that I'd been among the beaten), they came to me with their stories, both eyewitnesses and people in the neighbourhood, including clan members, who'd heard from others.

From them all, I pieced together the following story:

After the crew finished raising the flags, they went to the bar. And drank. And drank. And drank. For hours. According to some, triads were brought in from New Territories, maybe even from Yuen Long, to help locals erect the flags. It was part of the citywide, top-down effort. The drinkers waited for the culprit to return. Just about wherever you went in the neighbourhood, you had to pass by that main street: it was the perfect gauntlet. When, hours into their drinking bout, the young man they suspected of tearing down the flags finally came, they shouted at him.

Eyewitnesses said the thugs were incited by the woman whom I heard from my home yelling at them to beat him up. It was, they said, as if she were challenging their manhood, and they responded to that, setting upon him, punching him. He fell to the ground. They kicked him repeatedly. An older man attempted to intervene, and he became their next victim. I myself didn't see him that night. The other victim I did see, another young man, simply happened to be standing off to the side and was attacked for apparently no reason at all except that he happened to be there. There was a fourth victim as well, whom I didn't see either. In all, four were sent to hospital.

It was clear to me that the thugs' motive for the assaults was that they felt the tearing down of the flags was an unacceptable challenge to their power in the neighbourhood; someone had to pay.

*

The Party was like a conductor of an orchestra of violence. It preferred to leave the rough stuff to its proxies, the Hong Kong police and the bottom-feeding triads and thugs. It preferred to pretend to be above the fray. It preferred that its own violence remain mostly in the form of an implicit threat, the Party's army providing the ultimate backstop. Actually using that violence, sending in the army, for example during the Tiananmen Massacre, would be an admission of its failure to enforce compliance through less extreme means. But violence was always there. Violence worked best as a threat, when it was not used, just implied. You could be next, so you'd better be careful. It had a whole propaganda apparatus to intimidate, to instil fear, and means to make that permeate society.

I had had some experience of that. Not long after the protests began, the two Party-owned newspapers in Hong Kong published very similar articles about me. It was in the early days when the Party was still trying to figure out the most effective propaganda approach, and at that time, they were going with a classic, the "black hand": the protests were incited by a few black hands who were manipulating the masses behind the scenes. The articles included photos of me supposedly orchestrating demonstrations.

Nobody actually read those Party-owned newspapers in Hong Kong; the only circulation they had was as free street-corner giveaways to gullible people. Their function was not to reach a mass audience but to give the cue to Party allies on social media, who did have some reach, to kick into action. In the days that followed, mash-ups of those articles appeared on Facebook and in WhatsApp groups, often sprinkled with leaks of personal information such as ID number, phone number and even address.

The Party-owned papers stooped low, publishing a photo of my children. One social media post featuring that photo was reposted by the neighbourhood pro-Communist district councillor. Before long, I was getting a lot of long stares as I walked down the street. Men "accidentally" bumped into me. I heard swears behind my back. The last straw came when posters denouncing the black hand began to appear on lampposts around the neighbourhood accompanied by the photo of my children, in some cases with their eyes gouged out.

We left the neighbourhood and did not return for several weeks. When we did, it seemed that things had died down. These things came and went in waves. But I still felt like a marked man. This was why, when the flags were torn down and I was considered a suspect in the eyes of some, I knew to be on guard.

Only a few days after the assaults, as I was walking down the main street, three police officers passed. Two I recognised from the night of the assaults, one of whom swore at me out of the corner of his mouth. I stopped and asked what he'd said.

His colleague turned and approached me, shouting, "What's your problem? Do you have a problem with my colleague? What are you, a troublemaker? You think you know everything, don't you? Let me shake hands with you. Let me congratulate you on being so smart. Oh, you won't shake my hand? What's wrong with you?"

He kept coming towards me. I kept backing away. Everyone stopped to watch. His physically aggressive posturing reminded me of the man who'd shoved me on the 30th, the only real difference being that he didn't actually touch me.

"Aren't you going to answer me? Do you want to go to the police station and talk this over? I could bring you there."

"I just asked your colleague what he said to me. I don't think you are acting properly, so I am not going to stay here." I turned and walked away.

Not only were the police not going to pursue the culprits, they were going to hound the people who tried to get them to do their job. Everyone in the neighbourhood saw this; they stood watching us. It sent a clear message.

I told the WhatsApp group about it right away and

received a flood of support. It was when I saw those black angels coming to rescue me that night that I knew we had something special in the neighbourhood. After that, while I was ever vigilant, I never felt afraid. I knew they would have my back. There was virtually nothing the police or thugs could get away with.

Ming, the one who'd just announced she was running for District Council, suggested I meet the police Community Relations officer for our area. She had a good relationship with him and had always found him very helpful and forthcoming. She said the officers' behaviour on the street was unacceptable and needed to be reported. It was such a small incident that I didn't want to bother, but then figured that if anything were to happen to me later, it was important to have down on record that such incidents had preceded it.

The Community Relations officer contacted me, suggesting we meet. I told him not to bother coming all the way to see us. But he was so insistent, I began to suspect the purpose was to monitor me. I imagined they had some big file on me that he thought he could add to. Still, I agreed. Part of me wanted nothing to do with police, especially in that period. I wanted to keep as far away from them as possible; contact with them was dangerous. But another part was curious to talk with an officer.

Ming accompanied me to the meeting at a pro-democracy restaurant (our choice). Henry, the Community Relations officer, brought his young subordinate Matthew. Both were dressed in civilian clothes. They came from police headquarters, not the local station.

Henry told us the police station officer in charge (OIC) had "debriefed" the officers I'd encountered on professionalism and attitude. Of course, they denied the incident had occurred.

I thanked Henry for following up the matter. As far as I was concerned, it was closed. Henry actually wanted me to meet the OIC but she'd been reluctant. I told him not to push her; I didn't want to put her in an uncomfortable situation.

He then updated us on the investigation of the assaults. The case had been transferred for investigation to the Regional Crime Unit, out of the hands of the local police, as it was noted they had cordial relations with the community out of which the assailants were suspected to have come. There was a CCTV camera belonging to a bank exactly where the incident had occurred, and police were in the process of asking the bank to release the footage to them, which could take a matter of weeks. He was confident this would show everything that took place. Police had spoken with the victims at the hospital, but so far, none had made a formal statement. He asked me for my account. I gave it. The food arrived. The others began to eat. I didn't feel like eating.

The conversation drifted to the political situation. I said, "I sympathise profoundly with the police. I think they [I kept it in the third person rather than switching to the second, as if I weren't talking to cops] have been put in an impossible situation by the government, which is using them to deal with a political crisis. I think the police hierarchy has fallen into the hands of hardliners. They were promoted after Umbrella for their hardline views, and now they're the ones calling the shots."

Henry and Matthew nodded, as if in agreement. Then Henry launched. "I think they should just send the whole government back to China. China should take over. China isn't like it was before. China's better. China wouldn't change Hong Kong. It would leave it like before. It knows the world is watching."

Ming and I remained silent. We let him go on. He was building up steam.

"We have more freedoms now than ever. Do you think we had more freedoms under the British? They had political prisoners.

"I was born in Macau. When I was little, my parents brought me here. They thought I'd have a better future here. Hong Kong was better then. I never thought I'd see the day when Macau is better than Hong Kong. But that's what it's come to.

"The young people compare Hong Kong to Ukraine. They want Hong Kong to be like Ukraine. But you know what: 85 per cent of the women there want to get married to someone abroad so they can leave the country. You can go online and get yourself a Ukrainian wife whenever you want. The GDP is 1 per cent of what it was before. Women are selling their wombs for surrogate babies. Is that what we want here?

"And democracy: Look at Thailand. The military had to step in. All it brings is chaos."

I wondered what Matthew thought of his boss's rant. He looked ever so slightly pained, or maybe that was just my impression. He was such a gentle, thoughtful, sweet-looking young man. He reminded me of my daughter's primary school teacher. How did he end up in the police force?

The more Henry went on, the more reactionary he became. It was as if he couldn't stop himself; the words tumbled out. His speech was made up of the detritus that swirls in a closed environment, unexposed to critical comment or dissenting view, taking on a life of its own, increasingly divorced from reality. It was easy to imagine officers repeating these lines to each other endlessly, the same bits of information, misinformation, half-baked ideas all mixed together in a big jumble of irrationality and incoherence.

And Henry was one of the nice guys. He prided himself on his service-with-a-smile attitude, his ability to get along with others, his willingness to attempt to bridge the huge gap of distrust between police and citizens.

I couldn't quite tell what had provoked his rant; it felt like something he just needed to get off his chest. He must have known that people like Ming and me wouldn't agree with him. But he never stopped to ask what we thought; he just went on and on.

"Democracy only works with highly educated people. Hong Kong people aren't educated enough. They have no political education, no education about the country. Young people just pick a bit from here, a bit from there. They haven't sacrificed. You have to work hard to get something. They think they're working now but they're not."

My attention flagged. I saw Henry's face, saw him looking at me, saw his lips move, but heard no sound. I drifted off to a memory of a recent encounter.

✤

Three police officers in full riot gear have stopped a young man on a street corner. He is not masked. He is not dressed in black. He holds open a soft leather briefcase which they inspect.

These stop-and-searches of young people were routine: it was said being young had itself become a crime.

I film them with my camera at a distance of three or four metres. I want them to see me filming them. It's what I usually do when I come across this scene. For documentation purposes. To send the message, We are watching you; we don't approve; there may be a time when you will be held accountable; we will not be intimidated.

For that is what the stop-and-searches were meant to do, intimidate people, make them scared to walk the street, especially if they were young.

One cop notices me. He turns away from the young man and approaches. "What's your problem?" he says.

"Why did you stop him?" I ask.

"Not your business," he says. "Move along." I say nothing. I do nothing. I continue filming. "Do you know him?" he asks.

"No."

"Then you're invading his privacy," he says, motioning to my phone.

This statement was too stupid to merit a response, but it seemed to be what police had been advised by their superiors to say, since I'd heard it from several, the idea that somehow filming someone on the street as they were stop-and-searched by the cops was an invasion of their privacy, but cops stop-and-searching them was not. Cops posed as the protectors of the privacy of someone whose civil rights they were abusing.

"Move along or I could arrest you," he says.

"You should be nice to me," I say.

"Why should I be nice to you?" he says, parroting me.

"Because I'm your boss."

"You're not my boss."

"Who do you work for then?"

"You're not my boss."

"Don't you work for the people of Hong Kong?"

"You're not my boss." He waves me away dismissively

and turns back to the man they've detained.

"The people of Hong Kong are your boss, or should be. If we're not your boss, who is?"

As he turns to glare at me, his colleague whispers in his ear, probably telling him to ignore me. A crowd of several dozen has gathered around us. They are silent. I can feel they're on my side. They are to me as I am to the young man, watching, witnessing, doing what we can from our position of powerlessness to look after one another. You never leave anyone behind – a basic tenet of the movement. I can tell the police are beginning to sense they might have a problem. I've seen dozens of their colleagues patrolling the streets nearby, but none are in the immediate vicinity. If there were lots of them, they'd bully us. But since they're just three, they're starting to consider how to extricate themselves from this situation in which they're outnumbered.

"You shouldn't threaten the people who pay you," I say. "I'm a taxpayer. I pay your salary. You work for me."

"We're taxpayers too," several others shout.

"No taxation without representation," one person adds in English.

The police finish searching the young man and return his ID card to him. They walk past me, chests thrust forward, arms to their sides, taking as much space as possible, forcing me to move aside, just to show who's boss.

"Thank you, thank you," I say, as if they've let the man go to oblige me.

I'd told people to ask the police that question whenever the police threatened or intimidated them: who do you work for? It got to the crux of the matter. Of course, the police could say they worked for no one; they were charged with upholding the law, which was in the public interest, but that didn't address the way they routinely treated citizens as the enemy, or the fact that they were brutalising protesters agitating for their basic rights while working for the people responsible for denying them. Where else did you pay someone to beat you up?

But I didn't ask Henry and Matthew those questions. The longer I heard Henry talk – and he went on and on – the less I could bear it. I had to leave and was looking for a polite escape. I managed to interrupt him long enough to say my goodbyes, leaving poor Ming there to soak up the rant by herself.

*

Ming had the qualities of a good politician coupled with the heart of a good person. She could interact with anyone, listen to everyone, relate to everyone as one human being to another. She was inherently moderate; she wanted the best for everyone, including the people who didn't like her. We were lucky to have her as our candidate. We couldn't have hoped for a better one. Plus, I knew she would stand by me. If we couldn't win with her, maybe a pro-democracy candidate would never take this neighbourhood.

Not long after the WhatsApp group coalesced in July, the question of who would run in the District Council election arose. Finding someone and supporting them became our *raison d'être*; we were the campaign team even before we had a candidate.

All across Hong Kong, as the protests went on and the elections neared, there was a hunger to field pro-democracy candidates. The District Council elections, for which no one had shown much enthusiasm before, were seen as protest by other means, a de facto referendum on the protest demands, government repression and police violence.

I was and had always been ambivalent about them, as I was about elections in Hong Kong in general, because they were neither free nor fair; in fact, whenever the word was used here, it should be put in quotation marks or asterisked: "election", election*. They were meant to present the illusion that Hong Kong somehow had a semi-democratic system while withholding from the people any sovereignty or power. There was no democracy in Hong Kong. You either had democracy or you didn't, and we didn't. And to some extent, participating in elections*, participating in a rigged system, legitimised that system, even if one did so to bring about democracy.

The chief executive was selected by a committee of 1,200 electors, rigged to ensure it selected whichever candidate the Party preferred. Formally the chief executive was appointed by the Party and accountable to the people of Hong Kong, but in practice, it was only the master's voice that mattered. You could search long and hard and never find an issue on which the chief executive's policy departed from that of the ruler, even and especially when the majority of Hong Kong people opposed the regime, the extradition law and current protests being only the most recent case in point.

Fifty per cent of the Legco was elected according to principles of universal suffrage. These were the geographical constituencies. But the other 50 per cent was made up of so-called functional constituencies, again rigged to ensure that the majority would always do the bidding of the Party. And it wasn't even a true legislature, in the sense of being a law-making body: it could not propose legislation, only vet what was proposed by the government. For this reason, I refused to call them "lawmakers", a term often applied to them, borrowed from genuinely democratic systems in which the parliament really did make laws. They ran in elections* that were neither free nor fair so as not to be able to make laws.

Not only was the political system deeply undemocratic; it was also a failure. Hong Kong was a place in perpetual political crisis, but because it had a well-functioning, efficient civil service and disciplined people with a strong work ethic, it always managed to get by without a government to speak of. The people in those positions were simply there to obstruct, to fill space, to prevent anyone truly representative of the will of the people from filling them.

Then there were the lowly District Council elections. On the face of it, these were the most democratic. All but a few of the 452 seats in 18 District Councils were filled according to principles of universal suffrage. But the reason the people were allowed to elect whoever they wanted to those seats is that District Councils had no power. Essentially no more than advisory bodies, they were set up by the British colonials to give Hong Kong people the illusion of political participation without any power. At most, they gave people some say in local affairs. And 452 seats in a city of seven million?! There were so many that not even the richest, best-resourced pro-Communist party could run a candidate for every one of them. In every election, many seats went uncontested. While there had been a huge struggle for years over universal suffrage for the chief executive and Legco – that was what the Umbrella Movement was all about – District Councils had never really mattered, and most people had never paid them much attention or taken them that seriously; voter turnout was usually substantially lower than for the rigged Legco elections.

After the Umbrella Movement, there was a debate, especially among new post-Umbrella groups and young people, about whether even to take part in a rigged, illegitimate system. But eventually even those groups most sceptical of participation decided to run in the 2016 Legco elections. They did quite well.

Then the purge began: six democratically elected Legco members, all pro-democracy, were kicked out; more than 20 were put on trial. Between 2016 and 2018, more than a dozen candidates were barred from running in elections on political grounds. They tried to enter the system, and the system spat them out, proving just how rigged it was.

Shouldn't that have settled the matter of whether to try to operate within it or not? Let the traditional pro-democracy parties that had worked within the system for decades continue to do so and fight the good fight as best they could from the inside, but the rest of us? Should we really bother any more?

And how many would the government bar from running this time, given they'd barred dozens in the past three years, especially considering so many protesters and young people were running, precisely the sorts they'd disqualified before?

Yet hope, stupid hope, springs eternal. And for the first time ever, pro-democracy candidates would be running for every single one of the 452 seats. I could see the point, I supported them, I would campaign for them, but it was hard for me to get that enthused. Little did I know.

In our neighbourhood, there had never been a pro-democracy district councillor. Eight years before, in 2011, a shaggy-haired well-intentioned young man ran against the pro-Communist incumbent. He was from a party, League of Social Democrats, that many Hong Kong people back then considered radical, though in a European democracy it would have been considered, well, social democratic. I was on his campaign team. With no funding at all, he got 35 per cent of the vote, which I thought at the time was pretty good. Four years later, in 2015, the district councillor who'd been in power forever ran unopposed.

The District Council was a member of the Democratic Alliance for the Betterment and Progress of Hong Kong (DAB), the biggest pro-Communist party and pretty much its proxy. She had two nicknames: Ms Concrete and Ms Do-nothing. Both were appropriate. Her purpose was mainly to funnel government contracts to the construction and property bosses and to give them whatever political protection she could afford. Across the city, District Council seats were filled by people like her. Like their superiors in the Hong Kong government, they weren't there actually to do anything, just to occupy the seats so no one else could. They held a few banquets, gave out free calendars at New Year's, and that was about it; otherwise, you never heard from them though they had offices in the very neighbourhood where you lived.

And so you had the discrepancy: on the one hand, at least two-thirds of Hong Kong people wanted universal suffrage; on the other, all 18 District Councils were controlled by pro-Communists. Supporters of the regime – that is to say, people who backed it without getting any tangible benefit, such as profitable business connections (the tycoons) or power (the officials) – were disproportionately older, less educated, poorer and more inclined to vote. We had plenty who fitted into those categories in our neighbourhood. Why did they support the regime? It was hard to say. Out of a sense of being Chinese. Due to a deep-seated authoritarian streak. To preserve the status quo. As a reaction against change. Loyalty to the clan bosses. False consciousness: these people were at the bottom of a steeply tiered, grossly unequal economic and political status quo that the Party and its allies had every intention of maintaining.

So it was you could have a system that was thoroughly un- and even anti-democratic with some superficial trappings of democracy.

The candidate many in the WhatsApp group initially thought should run, a beloved shopkeeper and community leader, decided not to. The young assistant to a well-known and respected pro-democracy Legco member said that if no one else ran, she would. I thought she'd be a good candidate: she was bright, competent, energetic, politically savvy and well connected to other pro-democracy figures elsewhere in the city. But the team was sceptical. She was too young and had just moved to our neighbourhood – no one knew her, and whereas elsewhere in the city many twenty-something neophytes were running, our neighbourhood was an ageing part of the city, and the team figured there was a prejudice against youth that would be hard to overcome.

Then, only a few weeks before the official campaign period kicked off, Ming put her name forward. She was our saviour: it was hard to run a campaign without a candidate. A natural people person, she had a vaguely maternal air about her. And in her fifties, she fit the age profile most of the team were looking for.

Not only that, but her political instincts were well suited to our generally conservative neighbourhood. I was surprised when, one day out canvassing, only a week after the assaults and three days after she'd declared her candidacy, she told me she'd only recently "converted". She hadn't taken part in the Umbrella Movement or been that interested in politics in general. She had a good job at a publishing company and was offered a promotion and a big raise, but something made her hesitate. Most of the company's business came from the PRC, and the new position would mean working mostly with people from there. That made her uncomfortable. She got along with the Chinese fine and in fact was good at working with them, but felt somehow that she was betraying Hong Kong. She wanted to work with Hong Kong people. She asked her boss for three weeks' leave to think it over.

This was around the time the protests kicked off. She was inspired by the protesters and read everything she could, talked to whoever she could. It was a huge learning experience, a transformation, the kind one usually associated with youth, that time in life when a whole new world can open up to you. For that to occur, you have to be open and receptive in a way that not that many older people are. I gave Ming credit for that but also wondered how she could have been so naive, or maybe more accurately, oblivious. Then again, many were. As my partner often said, 40 per cent of people everywhere are idiots, a factor to contend with in any electoral politics or really in any political endeavour.

At any rate, from then on, there was no looking back. Not only did she not take the promotion, she resigned from her job. She didn't know what she would do instead, but it couldn't be that. She came from a blue family. Her parents and all her siblings were blue. She'd only just told them she was running for District Council. Some told her, "Be careful"; others said nothing at all.

Coming from that background, she understood the mentality of the blues and neutrals well: she came from blues, and until recently, she'd been something of a neutral herself. She could reach out to them, talk to them, speak their language, hear their concerns and respond empathetically. She was the sort who could win people over in a single encounter. I sometimes wondered if we wanted a candidate who was so new to the pro-democracy cause, so new to politics. But it wasn't as if we had much choice; no one else had volunteered.

Ming was so good at appealing to DAB voters on a personal level that she and others in the team even believed they might be able to get some of the neighbourhood's blues to defect. We agreed that there was general discontent with the incumbent, including among her base, but I was sceptical any would actually change sides. In our neighbourhood, a rock would get the number of votes the incumbent had the last time she faced a challenger, as long as the rock was from the DAB. I argued we shouldn't assume we'd make any inroads into her base but rather that it was fixed. If we were to win, we had to mobilise every last voter who wasn't part of that base to vote for Ming. That was achievable, if still a huge challenge, at this time like no other, because of the protests.

Elsewhere candidates were running explicitly as protest candidates, declaring their platform was the five demands and hardly mentioning local issues, District Councils' usual bread and butter. Ming was wary of positioning herself as a protest candidate alone, thinking that just wouldn't go down well in the neighbourhood. Her preferred profile was "the candidate for everyone", not just a few vested interests, the person who would bring the community together. She didn't have a lot of strong opinions and was open to persuasion on most issues. She often said, I'll work for what the majority wants. As much as running on a set of specific ideas or proposals, she was running on a democratic style of leadership.

Before she'd even formally announced her candidacy, just after the day of mourning at the start of October, we conducted a survey to ask people in the neighbourhood what their top priorities and issues were and what they wanted done about them. From the responses, Ming derived a 25-point platform. The process embodied participatory democracy. In a way, the whole point of the campaign, as much as winning, was to promote this. We wanted people to take control of their lives, to think differently about their relationship to government and feel empowered to participate in governance.

Out of those 25 points, only one was directly protest-related: the five demands, the last point, number 25, on the list. Even then, people, invariably the old and the cranky, would come up to me when I was out canvassing, point to number 25 on the flyer and say, I'm not voting for her because of this. But more important than any of those 25 was her promise to listen to everyone: she would not be the one forming the agenda; the people in the neighbourhood would; she would carry it out.

Ming was wary of having the big names in the pro-democracy movement come to our neighbourhood and campaign on her behalf, as they did elsewhere. She feared it might be divisive and alienating, creating a backlash. Of course, I wanted them to come. I thought she was being a little too cautious, but it was her call.

Our neighbourhood was changing. A lot of people who led what I called "intentional lives" had moved there in recent years because, well, those types of lives tended not to be so lucrative, and the neighbourhood, run down and scruffy, was one of the more affordable in the city with the least affordable housing on earth. (Nearly half of Hong Kong's population lived in government-subsidised public housing because it couldn't afford housing at market rates.) These were people for whom values and beliefs came first, and they tried to find some way to make a living that aligned with, responded to, or at least didn't betray those. They were our base, and they were enthusiastic about Ming. But there were lots of others who were just fed up with Ms Concrete Do-nothing and wanted something different. And there were plenty who were involved in the protests, and for them the choice was clear.

The campaign team was pulling together, not only as a force in the elections but also in the movement. We were developing our own culture, a way of living, of thinking, of acting, of collaborating. It was an exciting time. There was such great solidarity amongst us. When I went to the protests and my partner was away, people in the group babysat my kids.

I loved all the grunt work, like folding and taping circulars (election ads) to be sent through the post to neighbourhood residents, sitting around the big table with the others doing monotonous tasks, talking about all kinds of things. As ever, it was the middle-aged women who stepped up to the tasks.

There was Margaret, who worked for a Chinese investment firm. Whenever there were big weekday protests, the firm warned employees against taking sick days and monitored their presence at the office. But, she said, though no one dared talk politics at work, she thought most of the workforce, which was half Chinese and half Hongkongers was "light yellow". Even the Chinese? I asked. Yes, she said, they came to Hong Kong to get away from China; they don't want it becoming what they were escaping from. She never canvassed with us, confining herself to "back office" work (like folding circulars) and only protested fully disguised, for fear of losing her job.

There was well-connected Irene with the husky voice. She picked up the phone and ordered takeout; before long, a friend of hers appeared with the food. She picked up the phone and ordered campaign T-shirts; before long, a friend of hers appeared with boxes of them. It was an indispensable political organising skill, to know so many people so well you could count on them to do for you what needed to be done, from the big things to the small.

There was pensive Susan, who'd studied philosophy at a Canadian university. A good listener, she would hear what others were saying and then, just when one might think she hadn't been paying attention, so long had she been quiet, she'd make a remarkably astute comment that cut to the heart of the matter.

There was Maxine, so sweet I took her for naive. She resented me for that, I could tell. She'd grown up in the West. Her parents were immigrants from Hong Kong. She'd never lived in the city herself until an adult. I often thought people who came from stable democratic societies had great difficulty perceiving the true evil of dictatorship. They had a natural assumption that somehow, some way, whatever their foibles and even abuses, the authorities were working for the good of society. It made it hard for them to comprehend fully the zero-sum political struggle going on in Hong Kong. Maxine was so good-hearted, she assumed the best of intentions in everyone, a habit that when applied to CCP rule would simply lead you astray.

And foul-mouthed Dominique, whom I had known for

years as the unassuming widow of a prominent editor who'd died suddenly mid-career. The first swear sounded all wrong coming out of her mouth, but then I got used to it. "We must get rid of these blue objects," she'd shout over and over, walking down the street with me, surrounded by the "blue objects" we had to get rid of. She was satirising the police, who had infamously called a man dressed in yellow they had detained and kicked while he lay prostrate a "yellow object". She had a knack for coining incisively appropriate new phrases like that. I teased her about how revolutionary she had become. "Fuck the system!" she'd shout. "Fuck it! Fuck it!"

*

Then there was Agnes. Her child was born just a few days before mine in the same delivery room at a public hospital with a beautiful view of the sea. Agnes was a Christian of the render-unto-Caesar variety. She'd never shown any interest in politics. The closest she'd ever come to activism was circulating a petition against a lesbian character in the film *Frozen II*.

But the protests did something to her. She came alive, became the person she was meant to be, discovered that the life she'd been leading was simply too small for her. It started with a visit to a group of mostly Christian hunger-strikers outside government headquarters not long after the protests began. Then she put up the neighbourhood's first and only Lennon Wall. It was torn down multiple times, and a man posting a message there was punched in the face. She kept putting it back up and tending it. Her otherworldliness was transformed into calm fortitude.

She ran a small tea shop that also sold knick-knacks collected in large suitcases on trips to Japan. Schoolchildren loved to stop in and buy the elaborate Japanese erasers as treats for themselves when they did well on tests. It was a Hong Kong shop – laughably small: two people standing side by side with arms outstretched could reach from one wall to the other. It had its own Lennon Wall, festooned with multicoloured bright Post-it notes left by patrons. In another part of town that might have been unremarkable, but in ours it amounted to a brave statement of principle.

She was one of the first in the city to promote her shop as a "yellow" shop and later played a leading role in the burgeoning Yellow Economic Circle (YEC) initiative, the idea of which was, first of all, to discourage people from patronising businesses allied with the regime, and secondly, to buy from shops that supported the protests. Before long, apps were developed to help people locate both "blue" and "yellow" shops all over the city. Publicity campaigns educated people on YEC basics. A famous ad showed recognisable figures from the protests – the LIHKG pig, the lionbird, the Human Lennon Wall, Pepe the Frog – rendered into cartoon characters dancing to "Glory to Hong Kong" with a yellow hula-hoop around their waists, interspersed with different items that could be purchased from "yellow" shops.

There were different characteristics that made shops "yellow". Some showed public support to protesters. Some, like Agnes's, started their own Lennon Wall. Some restaurants provided free meals to protesters. Some sheltered them when police attacked. Still others were like homes away from home for young protesters who'd become alienated from their families over the protests. Some just didn't want to spend time at home because it was so unpleasant; others had been kicked out of the house by their parents. The shops gave them jobs. Some businesses specialised in providing vocational training to young protesters and helped them find stable jobs either at other "yellow" businesses or in the wider economy. The "yellow" restaurants and cafes were oases, gathering spots. You felt secure there, welcome, you could relax among your own. I called them "cultural multipliers" – they spread and entrenched "yellow" culture.

Of course, these "yellow" businesses represented just a tiny fraction of the overall economy – all the economic might was concentrated in the hands of pro-regime tycoons and Chinese state-owned Goliaths. "Yellow" shops were but a tiny David by comparison, but they acted as prominent ads for the culture of self-reliance. The YEC was not intended just to have an economic impact. Yes, it wanted to promote habits of consumption that were consonant with people's political ideals. But it was also part of a wider effort to develop a parallel society resembling the ideal democratic, egalitarian Hong Kong we envisioned.

Traditional economists said that the YEC could have virtually no economic impact on the city. But they were missing the point. To begin with, the protests of which the YEC was a part had already had an impact on the economy, affecting most every sector.

Some, like tourism, were especially hard hit. For years, tourism from the PRC had been promoted by the government as a key means to greater economic growth. Tens of millions of Chinese visited annually. Except for the few who depended economically on Chinese tourism, their presence in the city was very unpopular. Many malls and luxury stores that hardly any Hong Kong people patronised catered to them, reshaping central retail districts. Now that the protests had turned off the spout, many would be happy if the Chinese tourists never returned.

So it was possible that the protests had already begun to reshape the city economically. All the other so-called pillars of the economy were controlled by businesses allied with the regime, whether finance, trade or logistics, and it was true that the YEC would have little direct impact on them.

"Yellow" customers patronised yellow shops. It was the beginning, one hoped, of making Hong Kong a more economically self-sufficient place. Regime allies scoffed at the YEC: Ha, we get everything from China, including our water; what, so you want to use only bottled water from France now?! But economic dependence on the PRC was the result of regime policies intentionally designed for that effect; it was not inevitable, it could be reversed. Diversification of the economy was a goal worth working towards.

The boycott side of the YEC focused on businesses directly owned by the Party, such as state-owned banks, as well as Hong Kong businesses that had openly sided with the regime. These included large corporations such as the MTR, the city's subway system, which in August had begun to close stations near police-approved protests, presumably in an attempt to reduce turnout, and had continued to do so for months; and Hong Kong's flagship carrier Cathay Pacific, which had caved to Party intimidation and fired staff who had openly expressed support for the protests. There was also an #AnywhereButChina campaign afoot, the purpose of which was to discourage purchase of any products made in the PRC, not just ones sold at "blue" shops.

These initiatives sent a message: think about where your money comes from! Don't give your money to people who are helping to oppress you! This might seem obvious, but it was a surprisingly novel idea in Hong Kong. Ethical consumerism, ethical investment and the like had coursed through other societies, even if their impact was far too limited, but they hadn't much of a tradition in the city.

There was a general anti-consumerist strain to the protests, which I found encouraging. The attitude was, People are out in the streets fighting for our freedom; consumption of anything beyond the necessary is frivolous, even disrespectful. It wasn't just that fewer Chinese tourists were patronising Hong Kong shops; Hong Kong people themselves were shopping less.

Along with the tea and the Japanese knick-knacks, Agnes began to sell protest paraphernalia: flags, posters, art, banners, figurines.

Across the front of the shop was a row of miniature Lady Liberty statues. Lady Liberty was, like so much else in the protests, crowdfunded. A bunch of artists got together and made her. A towering figure several metres tall, she was strikingly different from her predecessors and inspirations, the Goddess of Democracy in Beijing in 1989 and the Statue of Liberty in New York. The latter two, however strong and resolute they may appear, were undoubtedly feminine, romantic symbols, objects representing concepts – democracy, liberty – to be revered. Lady Liberty, by contrast, was dressed in protest gear and held a "liberate Hong Kong, revolution of our times" flag. You couldn't even tell if she was male or female. Rather than a passive figure to be looked at and worshipped, she was a protagonist striding forward to bring about her own destiny. She would appear at various protests, stationary or borne through the streets. She was eventually carried all the way up the iconic

Lion Rock and left there, a supposed permanent home, looking beneficently down over the city like a guardian angel, but within 24 hours, she was vandalised, presumably by pro-Communists. The original spawned many replicas. The blueprints for 3D printing were circulated online and thousands of miniatures, like the ones in Agnes's shop, began to appear. Thanks to Agnes, the kids of the neighbourhood now had miniature Lady Liberties on their bedroom shelves.

If you were young and knew to ask her, Agnes would usher you into the tiny storeroom in the back of the shop to show you the equipment: gas masks, goggles, helmets. A high-quality set of protest gear could set you back hundreds of Hong Kong dollars, unaffordable to many young people, but Agnes, like many others, just asked the young protesters to pay whatever they could afford and assured them that if they could afford nothing, that was perfectly fine – it was her contribution to the struggle, just as their protesting on the streets was theirs. Everyone passed on their contributions like a chain of blessings, each linked to the next.

These secret storerooms had become all the more important after police raided places that openly sold gear to protesters, the most infamous example being the multiple raids on National Calamity Hardware. It sold wares legally available in other shops all over Hong Kong but because it was set up specifically to supply protesters, it became a police target. It had initially a traditional store in Sai Wan, but after that was raided, it took to opening pop-up shops in several locations, each lasting but a week or so, and inevitably raided.

Agnes even got child-sized protest gear for her kid. She took him to most protests, long after I'd stopped taking mine because of the danger of police attacks. They kept a safe distance from trouble, but you never knew. He was frequently photographed in his gear, and his likeness became an iconic protest image, reproduced on posters, found on Lennon Walls.

I wondered if she even sold any tea at all any more. She was always doing something protest-related and rarely spent time at the shop. Whenever I passed by, I saw young protesters she'd trained and hired part-time working there.

When the District Council election came around, she hung Ming posters all over the outside of the shop. Vandals at first scribbled curses on the posters in red. Agnes turned them into hearts. Then they tore the posters. Agnes hung them inside. Then they broke the large plate glass window where the posters hung. Agnes climbed a ladder and hung them as high up on the building as she could reach. The vandals didn't touch them after that.

I go out of my way to write about Agnes and the YEC to show that the freedom struggle was multifaceted. The protests got the lion's share of the attention, and indeed they were crucial, but the struggle had other important aspects – some liked to say three prongs.

Protests were prong one.

Prong two was community work, participatory grassroots democracy, participation in the rigged electoral system and the YEC – essentially the wider civil society, anything in Hong Kong outside of the protests.

The third prong was internationalising the Hong Kong issue: advocacy, lobbying and awareness-raising to that effect; cultivating allies and supporters abroad; pushing the cause higher up governments' foreign policy agendas; pressing for concrete action and legislation; and making the world see that Hong Kong was the front line of a global issue that would determine the outcome of the 21st century, the confrontation between open, free democracy and authoritarianism.

Together the three prongs formed a whole. Effective work had been done in each area. That such a coherent strategy had arisen out of a supposedly leaderless movement was remarkable. There was no one calling the shots, making the decisions. People just said, This needs to be done, and then took it upon themselves to make it happen.

The movement was made up of millions of Agneses, millions of black angels, all doing what they could. This was also what made it resilient, sustainable, hard to crush. I knew the protests would dissipate sooner or later; they had to – they couldn't keep going on like that forever. What would carry on the struggle once they did? The other two prongs had to be strengthened, so as to rise to the occasion when needed.

*

As the campaign went on, my attitude changed from ambivalence to excitement. Not for the first time during the protests, I realised there was so much I hadn't seen, hadn't understood. All of the new people running for District Council weren't entering into an impossibly compromised system and thereby also conferring legitimacy upon it; they were hacking it. They were turning the system against itself, as a means to democratise culture and society at the grass roots. If you had ever told me that one day District Councils would play an important role in the freedom struggle, I would have responded with derision. How wrong I had been – as long as we won.

The government had been insinuating that the elections might be postponed or even cancelled if "violence" didn't subside. It was expected that its allies, the pro-Communists, would get clobbered, and the only way to avoid that outcome was to not hold them.

Just as it was making those noises, the "violence" crescendoed, especially after the death of Chow Tsz-lok on 8 November, the ensuing Operation Dawn, which began on 11 November, and the police sieges of CUHK (12–13 November) and PolyU (18–29 November).

Then on 9 November, police arrested seven pro-democracy Legco members for an altercation with pro-Communist members over the extradition bill that had occurred in Legco way back in May. This was part of an ongoing crackdown on pro-democracy politicians and protest leaders that stretched back to the Umbrella Movement and had certainly not ceased with the recent protests, but still, the timing of these arrests was astounding: What was the government thinking? Either it really intended to postpone or cancel the elections and so just didn't care about the outrage at the latest round of arrests of democratically elected representatives, or it simply hadn't a clue.

Whatever the case, pro-democracy strategists couldn't stop laughing: either way, the government was screwed, was screwing itself. Cancel or postpone the elections and it would become even more unpopular in Hong Kong, and the whole world would note the anti-democratic turn; allow the elections to go on and it would get trounced, proving what we (and opinion polls) had been saying all along: we were the majority, they were an extremely unpopular tiny minority that could hold power only with the police, the Party and its army at its back.

Lose if they did, lose if they didn't was a prospect the government faced throughout the protest: on the surface, what one saw was the crackdown, the police brutality, the arrests, the march bans, the attacks on civil society, the paucity of clear protest victories. It was enough to get a protester down. But beneath the surface, the protests coupled with its own hardline refusal to negotiate or in any way recognise that protesters had raised issues that needed to be addressed, not dismissed, had boxed the regime in: it had no good options; and whatever it did, it risked tangling itself ever more tightly in a net set by the protests.

Then, suddenly, after 18 November, the first day of the police siege of PolyU, the "violence" stopped, a full six days before the elections. The government had no excuse to postpone or cancel now. And anyway, no protesters had ever threatened to target the elections. What could it do but let them go ahead while police besieged a public university and just after pro-democracy Legco members had been arrested?

Yet the result was far from a foregone conclusion. The pro-Communists, led by the DAB, had a formidable election machine with massive resources. Their supporters skewed old, and it just so happened that, as in many places, a far higher percentage of older people voted than younger.

Indeed, there had been signs that young people had given up on the system altogether. In 2016, the government kicked six democratically elected pro-democracy Legco members out of their seats. In the ensuing five elections (one case was still being fought at the High Court), pro-democracy candidates won just two seats. In one case, Lau Siu-lai, who'd been one of the six kicked out, tried to run to fill her seat and was barred from doing so. She was replaced by a veteran pro-democracy activist and politician,

Lee Cheuk-yan, a sure hand if ever there was one. And he lost. Because young people didn't come out.

So had the protests really changed everything? Would young people turn out? A good sign was that so many of the candidates this time around were themselves in their twenties. They looked, talked and acted like young people. The elections were regarded as an extension of the protests, and among protesters, it was considered one's duty to vote; not voting was simply not an option.

The day of the vote, across the city, people flooded the polls. In our neighbourhood, there were voting queues all up and down the main street for most of the day. Nothing like it had ever been seen before.

But they tapered off towards evening. Most had come out early amid rumours the government might close the polls early. I grew concerned, figuring we still needed a solid 2,000 more people to vote overall if we hoped to win. We'd run out of steam just when we needed a final push. We combed through the neighbourhood looking for people who hadn't voted yet but found only those who had and the unregistered.

As polls closed, we gathered in front of the polling station, our side at a set of tables out front of one restaurant, the other side at tables out front of the very bar where they were stationed the night of the assaults. Indeed, they were acting in much the same way. Even some of the same people were present, and the police were there as well. The tables were laden with large tubs of beer in ice. They got progressively drunker and more obnoxious as the counting went on. Right in front of the police, they threatened to riot if they lost. Meanwhile, we waited, patiently sober.

When the result was announced, they erupted into

applause. The pro-Communist had won, by 30 votes. It was so close, there was a re-count. Another wait. After the wait, the result was the same, except the margin of victory had increased to 35. Thousands of votes and we lost by 35.

From the last time there had been a competitive election in the neighbourhood eight years before, our vote count had increased by over 300 per cent; theirs had also increased, though only by 7 per cent, but that 7 per cent was enough to win. We gained a lot of ground but didn't quite get there.

The drunks hooted and hollered and lorded it over us, probably less dangerous than if they had lost. I smiled. The joke was on them. They were dinosaurs. Their days were numbered. By the time our election was called, the scale of the victory across Hong Kong could be surmised but was not altogether certain.

We left the vicinity of the polling station and retired to a nearby yellow restaurant to watch the results come in. By the middle of the night, it had become clear that a veritable pro-democracy typhoon had swept across the city. We won 86 per cent of all seats, 388 of 452 in all, more than tripling our wins, 124, in the District Council elections four years before, on a turnout of 71 per cent, the highest turnout in any elections of any kind ever held in Hong Kong, and that for seats that essentially had no power. That's how motivated people were to show the regime what they really thought. We won control of 17 of the 18 District Councils; the only loss was due to the fact that eight of the 18 seats on the council in question were ex-officio, not up for popular vote. Considering the political situation in the city, the pro-Communists had managed to mobilise their minority of voters remarkably well, just not well enough to get the results. While pro-democracy candidates won 86 per cent of seats, they got "only" 57 per cent of the popular vote versus 41 per cent for the pro-Communists.

The results, above all, were a vindication of all that we had been fighting for those many months. Throughout, the regime had said that the silent majority was with them, despite all evidence, including successive opinion polls, to the contrary. For the first time, the media could report without reservation or qualification that the majority of the city stood with the protesters and against the government and police.

But the victory wasn't only symbolic, as important as that alone was. For the first time ever, in the only almost fully democratic elections the city had, the pro-democracy side had taken full control of a level of government, the lowest, nearly powerless, to be sure, but it meant that it had a foothold inside the system and could use that as leverage against the regime. Beyond that, the councils were a platform to transform political culture, to encourage people at the grass roots to become more politically active, to help them to see that they could participate politically and have an impact, to make democracy take deeper root in every neighbourhood of the city. As I often said, if we only did politics as usual but a bit better, citizens would ultimately think we weren't that different from the opposition; we had to show we were qualitatively different in every respect, to give citizens a vision of the way a truly democratic city could be run. This was, potentially, the power of the powerless. If the new pro-democracy councillors made the most of the opportunity, citizens would feel empowered, would come to see that power, ultimately, was truly in their own hands. They would see that as long as we continued to resist, to stick together, we would eventually, however many long years it might take, win.

As their first joint action after the elections, the pro-democracy winners led a march the very next day to PolyU, where the police siege had entered its second week. Showing they were clearly on the side of the protests, they demanded the siege be dropped, the people still on campus allowed to go.

They would not formally take office until the new year, but already plans were under way: participatory budget for town-hall-style meetings; surveys on priorities; live broadcasts of District Council meetings for the very first time; publication of all documents related to agendas in a timely and transparent manner; investigations of controversial incidents the government and police had not made headway on, such as the thug attacks on citizens of 21 July in Yuen Long; attempts to hold officials accountable by inviting them to meetings; blocking government funding of local pork barrel projects; blocking funding for festivities related to the anniversaries of the PRC founding and the handover; sponsoring and protection of neighbourhood Lennon Walls (which the government had in recent weeks undertaken a concerted campaign to tear down but which communities wanted to preserve and maintain); and sponsoring of pro-democracy Chinese New Year markets after the government announced that, for the first time ever, no political groups or sellers of anything but flowers would be allowed to hold stalls at the government New Year markets.

*

Coming when they did, after more than five months of protests, the District Council elections were a watershed.

Four days later, the US president signed the Hong Kong Human Rights and Democracy Act into law, requiring the US government to impose sanctions on Hong Kong and Chinese officials found to have abused Hong Kong people's human rights and to assess annually the state of Hong Kong's autonomy, linking that assessment to the question of whether to continue the special trade relations between the US and Hong Kong. After months of protests, it was the first concrete, substantial measure taken by a foreign government in relation to the situation in Hong Kong and was widely celebrated by protesters. It was another kind of victory. It meant no immediate changes, and many suspected the US government might go light on enforcement, but it showed the rest of the world was watching, the most powerful country in the world, no less, and there were signs that the Party's reputation, at least in the West, was taking a pounding due not only to Hong Kong but to the concentration camps containing more than a million Muslims in Xinjiang and various other aggressive measures the Party was taking globally to gain greater influence.

We'd already forced the government to fully withdraw the extradition bill, the initial trigger of the protests. That, plus the landslide District Council elections victory and passage of the Hong Kong Human Rights and Democracy Act: not bad against the biggest dictatorship in the world, which from the start had signalled it would not bend. Not bad for this tiny little speck already halfway down the regime's throat.

A measured sense of accomplishment was mixed with feelings of failure and frustration. The outcome of the PolyU siege, with more than a thousand arrested, was regarded as a calamity, perhaps the worst so far for the protests. And all saw that, as far as we might have come, there was still so, so far to go.

Of the protests' five demands, withdrawal of the extradition bill was the only one that had been met. There had been no change in the Hong Kong government and no accountability for the fiasco of the extradition bill, in spite of the fact that the chief executive's approval rating was in the low double digits (14 per cent in a poll). There had been no acknowledgement on the part of authorities of the well-documented and systematic police abuses of protesters and of civil rights and no accountability for police abuses. In fact, just the opposite: the government and police, backed by the Party, were doubling down and taking a harder line than ever, attempting to intimidate and punish civil servants and teachers for their involvement in the protests, arresting thousands, prosecuting hundreds, banning marches, attacking even protests that had been given the go-ahead from the police. All expected that if the protests let up, the full force of the crackdown would be brought to bear. Legco elections were scheduled in 2020 and, like all previous ones, would not be held in accordance with the principles of universal suffrage, which meant, given their rigged nature, it would be impossible for the pro-democracy movement to gain control of Legco as it had of 17 of 18 District Councils. Meanwhile, the long-term strategy of the Party was the same as it had always been: to gain greater control over Hong Kong and assimilate it into the PRC, and the schedule for doing so was being stepped up.

The only way to head off the onslaught was to continue to resist, but that was easier said than done. Just how much longer could people keep it up? It was exhausting, and despite the resilient spirit of the movement, it was hard continually to motivate people with so few tangible goals to aim for in the near term, so little immediate prospect of success. You couldn't say victory was around the corner; all you could say was, if we keep fighting, we'll win one day. The future, as ever, looked uncertain, the struggle never ending. I didn't have the strategy that would bring us freedom; no one did.

❋

The day after the election, we went out into the main street at evening rush hour to welcome people back home and thank them for their support. It felt like a big party, complete with music. Uncle George played flute; Ah Ting played clarinet; Abraham, a young man who'd come from another part of the city to help us, played guitar. They bashed out protest hits like "Glory to Hong Kong" and "Do You Hear the People Sing?" Everyone sang along. Children danced. The black angels went about shaking hands, patting people on the back, congratulating them for a job well done. "We've come so far!" they said.

So many joined us that traffic slowed and then stopped. No one seemed to care that the street was blocked. Ming, trying to be the responsible member of society that you'd expect a now ex-candidate to be, did her best to reopen lanes to traffic, and slowly and intermittently, cars passed, honking their assent.

Some of the people coming home seemed taken aback. We were so happy, even joyful, but we'd lost, right? Yes, but it didn't feel that way. The rest of the city had won and even though we'd lost, it felt as if we'd won. "Thank you so much for your support!" "Keep up the struggle!" "This is just the start!"

We were partying in the very spot where the assaults had

occurred nearly two months before. There'd been no justice. The latest from Henry, the police Community Relations officer, was that the investigation had stalled. None of the four victims had agreed to give a statement. But we'd taken back the street, its own kind of justice.

In the coming days and weeks, neighbourhood violence didn't flare after the election, as I'd feared. In fact, it ceased entirely, even in its more muted forms. People no longer swore at me or "accidentally" bumped into me in the street. Both thugs and police backed off.

During the campaign, I'd often thought that if Ming lost, my days in the neighbourhood were numbered. The thugs would take a pro-Communist victory as the green light to go on the offensive. But their victory was so slim, and they'd been trounced so thoroughly throughout the city, that they were chastened, lying low, for the time being at least. I hadn't made any concrete plans to leave, and I thought – wondering at the same time whether I was just fooling myself – that however tenuous our security might be in that neighbourhood, it was our home; maybe we'd stick around a while longer.

SEE YOU AT THE POT

煲底見

See you at the pot!

– protest slogan

The protests spilled from 2019 into 2020. In December, 1.3 million protesters came out, more than in November, but fewer than in previous months. In January, it was 1.2 million. For the seventh straight month, more than one million Hong Kong people hit the streets to fight for their rights, bringing the overall number of protesters since the very first mega-march on 9 June to 14.1 million, nearly double the size of the population of the city. Where in the world had that ever happened before?

But the trend was downward. Of the 1.2 million protesters in January, one million attended the mega-march on the very first day of the year, about the same size as the first mega-march on 9 June. That means "only" 200,000 protested in the other 30 days of the month, and there was only one other protest in January that exceeded 100,000. The protests were losing some momentum, partly a victim of their own success. The government was desperately trying not to do anything too stupid, like banning masks or mass-arresting pro-democracy Legco members, so as to avoid provoking bigger protests. Meanwhile, the police crackdown was harsher than ever, with the ratio of the number of arrestees to overall protesters significantly increasing.

People were not giving up – the fact that as many people came out on 1 January as on 9 June showed that – but they were searching for the way forward. A movement needs short-term and intermediate goals to motivate people. First, there was the extradition bill. The government announced its withdrawal in September. Then there were the District Council elections at the end of November. The next tangible goal was Legco elections, but they were a long way off, not until September 2020. Meanwhile, there was no sign any of the other four outstanding demands would be met or even seriously addressed any time soon. Still, confronted with a vindictive government and brutal police, people persisted.

*

On 11 January 2020, Taiwan held its presidential and legislative elections.

Taiwan is the only Chinese-majority society that is a democracy. Hong Kong people regard Taiwan with admiration and envy. It's what they hope Hong Kong one day will become.

In the year preceding the elections, the Party pressured Taiwan, threatening it with invasion. It appeared to have an almost visceral antipathy towards Taiwan's president, Tsai Ing-wen, her very existence an affront. It regarded her as a separatist and Taiwan itself as a renegade territory. Xi Jinping proposed "reunification" on the basis of "one country, two systems", the very same arrangement in Hong Kong. If the fight against the extradition bill was about anything, it was a rejection of the constant push towards one country and away from two systems that has characterised CCP rule in Hong Kong for years. And yet this was what Xi was offering Taiwan.

Taiwanese watched the Hong Kong protests. They understood what we were fighting for and what we were up against. They were probably our biggest supporters. Many solidarity rallies were held in Taiwan. Upwards of 200 Hong Kong protesters sought refuge there and were taken in with open arms. Few Taiwanese people wanted unification of any kind with a Party-ruled PRC, and fewer still on the basis of "one country, two systems". The last thing they wanted to become was another Hong Kong.

Before the Hong Kong protests, Tsai had been down in the polls. Many were sceptical she could get re-elected. In local elections in 2018, the opposition Kuomintang, which advocated closer ties with the PRC, had made substantial gains.

But on 11 January, Taiwanese people re-elected Tsai and returned her Democratic Progressive Party (DPP) to a large majority in the Legislative Yuan. It was not a narrow win but a landslide victory, much like the November District

Council elections in Hong Kong for the pro-democracy movement. Influenced by Xi and the Hong Kong protests, Taiwanese people emphatically decided Tsai and the DPP were the ones who'd best defend Taiwanese sovereignty. Every time the Party's policies came before a vote by the people in the places it laid claim to, whether Hong Kong or Taiwan, it lost big.

*

That was the fourth victory of the Hong Kong protests, after the defeat of the extradition bill, the landslide District Council election victories and the Hong Kong Human Rights and Democracy Act and PROTECT Hong Kong Act becoming law in the US. Not bad for a small people in a tiny place up against the world's biggest dictatorship.

But what would winning – *really* winning – look like? Not just the consolation prize but the real thing. Not just preventing the worst from happening, but realising the vision of the best.

It would look like genuine universal suffrage in elections for the chief executive and Legco. It would look like an independent commission of inquiry into government rights abuses and police brutality. It would look like the cessation of mass arrests and prosecutions of protesters. Those in themselves would be major accomplishments.

But beyond those scenarios that correspond to three of the five demands, the most positive vision of victory is this: a free, open, democratic society over which Hong Kong people have control, about which Hong Kong people make decisions, with the promised high degree of autonomy.

The fuller positive vision looks something like this:

a Scandinavian-inspired country on the tip of China, an egalitarian social democracy. Scandinavian countries are the most perfect societies human beings have ever created in terms of democracy, equality and the general wellbeing of their citizens. Hong Kong's population is about the same size as those of the Scandinavian democracies. Like them, its people are highly educated and relatively homogeneous. About two-thirds of Hong Kong people subscribe to values and beliefs similar to those which are the bedrock of the Scandinavian democracies. It should be possible.

*

And yet it feels like a pipe dream. Not only is there the small matter of how to get democracy and autonomy while under the rule of the biggest dictatorship in the world, there is also the fact that Hong Kong is a thoroughly neoliberal turbo-capitalist economy, one of the most grossly unequal developed societies in the world. That doesn't mean it is impossible to get there, just that there is a very long way to go. Still, it's good to have something to aim for.

Most Hong Kong people would settle for democracy and autonomy and leave the matter of how to organise our economy for later. Of course, we would have to face the fact, sooner or later, that economic power is concentrated in very few hands in such a way as to undermine democracy. In this sense, Hong Kong is far closer to South Africa than to Scandinavia. When majority rule was achieved in South Africa in the early '90s, Nelson Mandela decided it was best for the time being to make friends with the white business establishment that dominated the economy. Two decades later, little has changed, apart from the fact that there is now a class of black mega-rich getting its share of the spoils, and the ruling African National Congress is both corrupt and entrenched.

One in six Hong Kong people want independence. A great many more fear that there is no other way of bringing about democracy and autonomy under CCP rule. At any rate, the prospect, however unlikely, raises the near-future question of whether, after these protests, so enormous in their scale and impact, Hong Kong can ever go back to the way it was before. One senses that it is entering a new phase. It is too early to say exactly what will define that phase, but that something has ended is clear: the supposed arrangements meant to be Hong Kong's governing principles, such as "one country, two systems", have proven unworkable. Hong Kong exists in perpetual political crisis, ruled by an illegitimate and unelected government. Sooner or later, something's got to change.

The conventional wisdom among China watchers is that there's no winning against the biggest dictatorship in the world, intent as it is on control and maintaining its monopoly on power. That seems a safe enough assumption, but the problem with that way of looking at the world is that, if the world conformed to it, it would never change. And yet the world does change. And will presumably continue to do so. So the question is less whether Hong Kong's situation will change, and more what will change and what will bring that about?

Again, the safe assumption is that the Party will continue to strangle Hong Kong more or less gradually until it has full control and the city is fully assimilated into the PRC. But then that hasn't been going well so far, has it? In fact, if anything, what's most striking is the mess the Party's made of it. It would be hard for it screw up any more than it has: a city in open rebellion for eight months, 22 years after it's passed into its possession. It's had 22 years to make it right, and this is what it's come to.

The safe assumption goes against the grain of the history of Hong Kong under Party rule so far, but it's reinforced by the perception that the Party is so powerful and the PRC so huge that by simple force of gravity, Hong Kong will be worn down to nothing: all the Party has to do is continue to apply the pressure. Of course, there will be some hiccups along the way, which is to be expected, but in the end, it will get its way.

Is this scenario any more likely than a variety of others, all of which depend on a number of variables that are difficult to predict? The world in general appears to be in rather large flux. So does the situation in not only Hong Kong but also the PRC. Will a Party-ruled PRC still exist in 2047, the end of the 50-year period of one country, two systems? Will one country, two systems last that long, especially considering the exacerbated and unresolved tensions of these last few years? Will the PRC simply gobble up Hong Kong long before then? Will Hong Kong even exist in 2047, whether in its current form or any other? The Party has the goal of subsuming Hong Kong as we know it under a larger entity, the Greater Bay Area, in the hope that Hong Kong will eventually become indistinguishable from the rest of the region.

*

The question of an ideal Hong Kong, as articulated earlier, is difficult to separate from the question of an ideal China. As much as many Hong Kong people may wish simply to have nothing to do with the PRC at all, the PRC won't go away, and whatever becomes of Hong Kong will be related to what becomes of China. From the point of view of the Hong Kong freedom struggle, the ideal China would be highly federated if not smaller. It would be best if whoever is to lead China agreed to Uighurs, Tibetans, Taiwanese and Hong Kong people holding referenda on their political status. After all, none freely agreed to be part of the PRC in the first place; all except Taiwan were swallowed up. If they are to be under the sovereignty of a Chinese state, then it must be by the formal consent of the majority of people in those areas and with a genuinely high degree of autonomy.

Of course, this vision is virtually impossible to reconcile with the reality of a Party-ruled PRC, even in its most liberal periods. The Party has promoted a virulent nationalism, blind to the concerns of others, in a hermetically sealed environment of propaganda and censorship. Even if the PRC were to become a democracy tomorrow, it is unlikely the Chinese majority would simply say, Of course, Tibet, Taiwan, Hong Kong and Xinjiang should be free. As long as the Party remains in power, about all one can realistically expect is a continued hardline and constant tensions with the peripheries. The situation appears intractable.

Hong Kong's best hope may be to thread the needle of change as opportunities arise. But how?

It's worth keeping in mind that, far from being omnipotent, the Party faces significant challenges; first and foremost, a slowing economy after decades of very rapid growth that has probably been the number one reason it's stayed in power. In theory, there is no reason the Party, with all the resources at its disposal and a massive propaganda and censorship apparatus, shouldn't be able to negotiate a slowing economy. The thing is, the PRC's economy is not only slowing but also transitional: most believe the recipe for growth up to now won't continue to succeed in the future. The Party has made efforts to shift away from that model of manufacturing for export and massive state investment, but the kinds of reforms that many economists deem necessary are nowhere in sight because, in order to undertake them, the Party would have to relinquish its grip on parts of society and the economy which it is loathe to do.

The international trade and economic environment has also become trickier. The Party devised initiatives such as Belt and Road in order to aggressively seek greater influence over wide swathes of the world, especially those in closest proximity to the PRC. Belt and Road has now caused significant blowback and in most cases failed to pay off in substantial material gains for the places it was supposed to impact positively. Most large Belt and Road agreements have been made with authoritarian regimes or countries with weak or flawed democratic arrangements like Pakistan and Sri Lanka. As an effort to reshape the world in its image – development first, power retained in the hands of the few – Belt and Road seems to have arrived at its limits.

But of course, Chinese money continues to have growing influence, and not only in the economically less developed parts of the world. There are plenty of signs of the Party's influence in the West as well. Its brand of authoritarianism oozes in through the cracks of free societies, gradually corroding their values and institutions. This is a new phenomenon that free societies are ill prepared to recognise, let alone contend with: never in modern history has there been an authoritarian state with such great economic influence on the rest of the world. Authoritarianism enters free societies by way of financial and technological influence; through Western corporations' willingness to censor themselves and their customers in order to curry favour with the regime; through telecommunications systems made and operated by Chinese companies close to the regime; through universities that have come to rely so much on the revenue from Chinese students that they're willing to allow Party influence to affect academic freedom; through academic journals and scholars willing to censor themselves and others; through basketball stars who love freedom close to home but disparage those fighting for it far away. It influences discourse and actions, shifting and subverting existing standards. If you don't pay attention, you'll look up one day and the society you thought you had is gone.

And yet probably more than at any time since Tiananmen, the perception of the Party appears to be souring. There is the trade dispute between the US and the PRC. The European Union has begun to recognise the PRC as a "competitor" (threat) rather than a "partner" (ally). The Party's actions in Xinjiang and Hong Kong and threats to Taiwan have come with some reputational cost. Everything – from Confucius Institutes to Chinese state propaganda organs abroad, to the Party's influence over diaspora communities, to Huawei and other PRC tech and communications companies closely allied with the regime – is coming under increased scrutiny.

The world is becoming more aware of the threat the Party poses. But that is hardly reassuring: it's taken its eye off the ball too many times before. It is suffering under particularly weak, ineffectual and cowardly political leadership. The regime will hardly go down without a fight. Dictatorships and authoritarians know how to play on the worst in human nature – greed, fear, selfishness, hatred – and leverage that to their benefit. The depths to which humans can stoop is well documented, and that all plays into the hands of the regime. Its wealth was built on Western businesses and politicians making self-interested arguments about how "engagement" would make China "more like us" and short-sighted, sleepwalking Western consumers who only cared about all the cheap made-in-China stuff they could get.

The Party's high-wire act will succeed only if we let it. It is not a foregone conclusion the regime in particular and authoritarianism in general will lose. It's up to us to ensure that. This responsibility is not a burden; it endows us ordinary people far from power with agency. The future of the world does indeed depend on us.

✹

There's no better example of that than in Hong Kong over the last eight months. No one can save our home but us. It is up to us to become more aware of the challenges and headwinds the Party faces, of its weaknesses, and exploit them to our advantage. Through the protests of the past eight months, we have achieved great internal unity and solidarity across a wide spectrum of ages, generations, political perspectives and ideologies. This is a great strength. We must work to preserve it, cultivate it, develop it. The regime, naturally, will try to drive us apart and fracture the movement. It's failed miserably at that up to now, but we must remain vigilant. The Party wants to exhaust us, make us quit, grind us to dust. It's huge and we're small. We can't let it. We have to find joy in the spirit of resistance. It must be central to our identity.

We must continue to develop civil society as the primary

vehicle of resistance. The 135 new labour unions that have arisen as a result of the protests are just one cause for hope. Forces such as these will keep us going when this phase of protests ends, helping us through the inevitable rough periods and troughs. Through both direct intervention and its United Front operations, the regime has attempted to make incursions into many different areas of society in recent years: the media, education, the judiciary and legal system. Wherever it does so, we must stop it in its tracks. It long ago captured the top echelons in Hong Kong: the government, the tycoons, the levers of the economy and many of the business, cultural, political and social elites. But we have to ensure that it will make no further inroads, however much it tries.

We have to continue to cultivate foreign friends and allies and to advocate for Hong Kong abroad. We have improved immensely in this area, but there is still a long way to go. Foreign governments have been reluctant to take up our cause and support us, but in this respect, we're hardly alone: foreign support has been lacking for just about every freedom struggle the world over. Perhaps it should go without saying, but what is meant by foreign support is certainly not military intervention but clear and vocal moral support, and, where appropriate, the enactment of laws such as the Hong Kong Human Rights and Democracy Act and the placing of the values of democracy, human rights and freedom at the centre of foreign policy. They should be reckoned into deliberations and agreements in areas of trade and business as in everything else. While governments have been reluctant to take tangible, substantial action, many people abroad have shown great support for us. People far away understand our struggle better than ever, including influential people in politics and the media. The foreign policies of free societies must become more responsive to the views and values of their peoples and perhaps less to business and trade interests.

And we have to persevere. We have to understand that this is a long-term struggle and the only way we'll win is by sticking with it. The culture of resistance that has developed up to now must become the bedrock of our existence. The regime must know that if it messes with us, there will be a fight. We must make it calculate the costs and downsides of any potential attacks and incursions it may be considering. Of course, this also means we must be willing to pay the price – the persecution and repression that are certain to follow.

A huge part of this strategy consists of waiting out the regime. It may let down its guard, make mistakes, weaken or even collapse, and when it does, we must be prepared to take advantage of that. We don't have the power to bend it to our will now, but that doesn't mean we don't have the power to outlast it; we do. The Party believes time is on *its* side. It may be right, but both its success and ours, mutually exclusive, depend on global shifts.

*

Our chances of success are much higher in a world in which democracy, human rights and freedom have the momentum, not when they are in retreat or decline, terms frequently used to describe their state in the past decade. That means people in democracies must elect leaders who will strongly and vocally advocate for those values, not through military adventures but through diplomacy.

If regimes like the CCP know democracies really take

democracy, human rights and freedom seriously and will fight for and defend them, that knowledge will affect their calculations. Right now, they know that in foreign affairs, democracy, human rights and freedom are at most an afterthought, something to which democracies pay lip service and perhaps consider once the trade and business deals have been struck. The downgrading of environmental and labour standards, the second-class status of issues like democracy, freedom and human rights, the primacy of trade and business have been ongoing trends since the rise of the World Trade Organization and neoliberal globalisation in the '90s. By now, they have become virtually a diplomatic reflex.

In 2019 alone, besides Hong Kong, there were major uprisings in Algeria, Sudan, Venezuela, Lebanon, Chile, Iran, Iraq, India and France. At root, most were struggles against authoritarianism. That is the root of the Syrian war as well, where, as I write, 900,000 people are fleeing a military offensive by the Syrian army and Russian air force in Idlib. Syria and its closest allies, Iran and Russia, are authoritarian regimes. The response of the world's democracies has been instructive: their greatest concern has been to keep fleeing Syrians out. This does not reflect well on the world's will or capacity to stand up for the basic values that not only make for a decent, fair society but are most likely to bring peace, stability and material sufficiency.

The state of both Hong Kong and the world is finely balanced. To put it simply, if the world becomes more democratic, we will win; if it doesn't, we may be doomed.

If we continue to cultivate all the strengths displayed in the protests; if we develop our resistance; if we persevere; if the Party continues to face headwinds and its international reputation continues to worsen; if the Party fails to deal effectively with the challenges it faces; if citizens of democratic states elect leaders who strongly and vocally advocate the values on which they are based; if there is a shift in the international climate in favour of democracy, freedom and human rights; then one day we will win.

It might sound like a long shot, but more unlikely things have happened.

✽

I can't recall when it was, but quite early in the protests, a saying began to circulate: 煲底見. When I first heard it, I didn't understand what it meant: "See you at the pot"? On its face, it wasn't the most stirring of slogans. It took me a while to realise that "the pot" was the nickname of a part of the Legislative Council building because of its vague resemblance to that kitchen item. "See you at the pot" was the very Hong Kong version of *¡Hasta la victoria siempre!*, except that, while the latter expresses militant resolve, "See you at the pot" envisions a dream.

Not long after I started hearing that, I saw a cartoon that depicted it. In the lower right-hand corner, two frontliners in full gear are crouched and alert, as if awaiting an attack. One of them turns to the other and says, "Promise me we'll win together." Thought bubbles emanating from his head lead to a vision that covers the whole rest of the page. Everyone is gathered outside the pot. There's a countdown: 4, 3, 2, 1. At zero, masks come off. The two who were on the front lines together point at each other and laugh, as if to say, "So that's what you look like?!" Someone speaks: "We welcome the release of all prisoners, we honour the memory of all martyrs." There's a salute. And then everyone cries, overcome with a mixture of sorrow at what has been lost and sheer incredulous joy: we've won. That's what "See you at the pot!" means.

In early October, when the protests were at their most intense, someone posted the following question on social media: "After we liberate HK, what will you do?" It elicited thousands of responses. Many were related directly to the protests, but others were simply visions of a worthy, meaningful life. Some expressed a desire to foster a greater sense of community among people, to share with others, to help others. In this, I recognised a vision of the new Hong Kong society: it would be much more caring, much less cut-throat. Typical of Hong Kong, a lot of the responses had to do with food and starting small businesses. Strikingly, none were particularly ambitious, at least in the widely understood sense of the word.

"I want to be an anthropologist, to study Hong Kong's eating and drinking culture, university halls' residence culture – what it means to be a HK person. I want to open a diner and pass on secret recipes for making milk tea and flaky egg tarts."

"I am a social worker! I want to make a big family, accepting people in need from ages 0-28. I see so many people who do not have warmth in their lives; it breaks my heart. I want to let them know that in this world, there are many people who care about them!"

"I want to open a bookstore. Every day, there will be a storytelling time, so that I can read to kids who visit. The bookstore doesn't have to be big; it can be small. Everyone can sit together, read and talk."

"I want to be a freelance writer and defend traditional

Chinese and Cantonese."

"If I am able, I want to open a care home for the elderly, so that our elders can have a good and peaceful place to live out their lives."

"I'm actually a baker. I want to open a bakery and an animal shelter."

"I want to be an accountant. I want to tally the crimes that the Hong Kong and Chinese governments have committed against us."

"I want to open a small shop and sit at the entrance every day saying hello to the people where I live!"

"I want to cook good and cheap congee, with special discounts for those who do not have a home to go back to!"

"I want to tell children the story of how their brothers and sisters fought for them."

"I want to be a farmer. I want to have a small restaurant next to the farm that only takes one table per night and people can pay whatever they like. Since you can't really plant things in the summer, we'll put on a musical every summer holiday."

"I want to open a cheap version of Subway."

"I want to make films, to document the beating pulse of the city, the joys and sorrows of its residents. I want to use the power of the camera, alongside music and narration, to tell stories that will inspire hope and love in people's hearts.

"I want to open a fishball stall. Because I like eating curry fishballs."

"I want to be the wife of a frontline protester."

"I want to open a stationery shop. In the past, I always stopped at the stationery store after school on my way home."

"I want to meet every single person who has helped me in this movement and be friends with them."

"I want to start an organisation that helps families with children with special educational needs."

"I want to be an archivist and record the history of us Hong Kong people."

"I want to sit down and listen to every single young person's story of resistance."

"I want to open a shop that sells cruelty-free and sustainable products and take responsibility to ensure that the Earth can be sustained for the next generation."

"As a gay person, I hope that after there is universal suffrage, we can achieve equal rights for all LGBTQ+ people, including the right to same-sex marriage."

"I want to open a museum that documents the history of Hongkongers."

The person who originally asked the question was overwhelmed by the responses and said, "Remember this feeling. Our tireless efforts today are all aimed at this: creating the best possible life. When you feel despair and feel like you are ready to give up, think about our lives after we win this fight."

Someone else, a Hong Kong person who lived abroad, asked, "But why can't you do those things now?"

That's just the point. For most, it's impossible in the society in which we live. Rather than struggle to realise those individual dreams, we've put our lives on hold to fight for our common dream. We know that it is only if we can achieve that common dream that we will be able to realise our individual dreams. We realise we live in an abnormal society, an oppressive society. We can't tolerate it any more. We won't stand for it. We deserve better. All we want is to live normal lives in a normal place. That is what we're fighting for. That is what winning would look like. Is it too much to ask? Here and now, perhaps. It does indeed feel like a dream, but a beautiful dream, a dream worth fighting for.

May it one day be realised.

See you at the pot.

APPENDIX

A TIMELINE OF THE HONG KONG PROTESTS

The first protest against the extradition bill occurred on 31 March 2019, but the Hong Kong protests are generally considered to have started with the first mega-march of 1.03 million protesters on 9 June. Protests continued over eight months up until January 2020, with at least one million protesters taking to the streets every month. With the onset of the pandemic, there was a lull in protests, but they flared up again from May to July 2020 in reaction against the impending imposition of the national security law, which came into effect late in the evening of 30 June 2020. Early July saw the definitive end of the protests which had begun more than a year before. In all, from 31 March 2019 to 3 July 2020, there were at least 1,099 protests and 15,216,581 protesters.

The massive protests were accompanied by an extraordinary array of events and developments related to them. This timeline is extensive but far from comprehensive and is meant merely to indicate the most important protests and events. It should not be construed as a coherent narrative history but as a point of reference. It includes all of the 34 protests of more than 100,000.

| HONG KONG PROTESTS BY MONTH, 2019-2020 ||||
MONTH	PROTESTS	PROTESTERS	PROTESTS WITHOUT CROWD ESTIMATES
MARCH	1	12,000	0
APRIL	1	130,000	0
MAY	0	0	0
JUNE	12	3,258,900	0
JULY	16	1,736,900	0
AUGUST	44	2,676,981	17
SEPTEMBER	338	1,439,025	269
OCTOBER	134	1,540,310	83
NOVEMBER	146	1,052,640	50
DECEMBER	112	1,366,285	0
JANUARY	33	1,272,238	0
FEBRUARY	52	20,902	0
MARCH	14	4,710	0
APRIL	6	1,500	0
MAY	46	363,670	0
JUNE	46	190,120	0
JULY	3	150,400	0
TOTAL	1,099	15,216,581	419

2018

17 FEBRUARY

A 20-year-old Hong Kong woman, Poon Hiu-wing, is murdered in Taiwan. Her boyfriend, 19-year-old Chan Tong-kai, later returns to Hong Kong, confesses to the murder and is arrested on 13 March, but he cannot be charged with murder because Hong Kong doesn't have jurisdiction over crimes committed outside Hong Kong. He is eventually charged with four counts of money laundering for taking and using her bank card.

2019

15 FEBRUARY

Citing the Poon Hiu-wing murder case, the Hong Kong government's Security Bureau submits a proposal to the Legislative Council to amend the Fugitive Offenders Ordinance and Mutual Legal Assistance in Criminal Matters Ordinance. This proposal is commonly referred to as the extradition bill. Its main purpose is to legalise extradition to jurisdictions with which Hong Kong has no extradition agreement. This includes the People's Republic of China, but not Taiwan, as Taiwan is not recognised as a separate jurisdiction by Hong Kong or the PRC but rather as part of the PRC.

31 MARCH

Twelve thousand attend the first protest against the extradition bill, a march organised by Civil Human Rights Front (CHRF), a veteran pro-democracy group that has been responsible for many large protests over the years.

3 APRIL

The Fugitive Offenders and Mutual Legal Assistance in Criminal Matters Legislation (Amendment) Bill 2019, or extradition bill, is tabled at the Legislative Council.

24 APRIL

Eight of the Umbrella Movement Nine are sentenced for various "inciting public nuisance" crimes related to the start of the Umbrella Movement in September 2014. Two are given eight months in prison and two others 16 months. The latter are by far the longest prison sentences ever in Hong Kong for non-violent protest. One of those two, Professor Benny Tai, is granted bail on 15 August to appeal his sentence. The other, Professor Chan Kin-man, continues to serve his sentence throughout the protests.

28 APRIL

One hundred and thirty thousand attend the second protest against the extradition bill, also organised by CHRF. It is the largest protest in Hong Kong since the Umbrella Movement in 2014.

29 APRIL

Confessed murderer Chan Tong-kai is sentenced to 29 months in prison after pleading guilty to four counts of money laundering. Because he has been remanded in custody since March 2018, he is eligible for early release in October.

9 MAY

Taiwan objects to the Hong Kong extradition bill and says that if it is passed, it will not seek the extradition of Chan Tong-kai or accept extradition arrangements with Hong Kong. Taiwan fears that if the bill becomes law, Taiwanese nationals could be extradited from Hong Kong to the PRC.

20 MAY

The Hong Kong government withdraws the extradition bill from the Legco Bills Committee, bypassing normal procedures in order to circumvent obstructive manoeuvres by pro-democracy Legco members and expedite it. It is scheduled for a second reading at a full Legco session on 12 June. On 21 May, chief executive Carrie Lam says the bill must be passed before Legco's summer recess.

30 MAY

In order to allay concerns expressed by civil society, in particular business groups, the Hong Kong government announces it will amend the extradition bill to reduce the number of extraditable crimes and raise the threshold for extradition to crimes punishable by seven or more years in prison. To most people, the changes appear cosmetic.

4 JUNE

One hundred and eighty thousand attend the annual candlelight vigil on the 30th anniversary of the Tiananmen Massacre, one of the largest turnouts in years.

6 JUNE

Three thousand lawyers dressed in black hold a silent march against the extradition bill.

9 JUNE

About 1.03 million people take part in the first mega-march against the extradition bill. Even before the march is finished, the government announces it's going ahead with the bill as scheduled.

12 JUNE

One hundred thousand surround government headquarters to prevent Legco from proceeding with the second reading of the extradition bill. With protesters blocking the entrance and exit, Legco postpones the reading. Police attack the peaceful protest, dispersing protesters and committing multiple abuses. The police commissioner labels protesters "rioters", a term with serious implications in Hong Kong law. The issues of police brutality and excessive use of force and of how the government and police employ the charge of riot with political motivation will become central to the protests.

13 JUNE

Legco announces the cancellation of the second reading of the extradition bill. No date for a vote is set. On 11 June, the Legco president said debate on the bill would finish by 20 June with a vote to follow. That plan is now scrapped.

15 JUNE

Chief executive Carrie Lam announces a "pause" or suspension of the "current legislative exercise" on the extradition bill. Echoing the words of the police commissioner, she calls 12 June protesters "blatant rioters".

In the evening, 35-year-old protester Marco Leung Ling-kit falls from the roof of the Pacific Place shopping mall near government headquarters, the first fatality of the protests.

16 JUNE

Two million people march, the largest protest in Hong Kong history. They take over many of the streets of Hong Kong Island between Causeway Bay and Admiralty. Police presence is minimal.

18 JUNE

Protesters make four demands that emerged from the 16 June protest and online discussion: 1. Completely withdraw the extradition bill; 2. Investigate the police force for brutality; 3. Fully retract the characterisation of the 12 June protest as a riot; and 4. Free all arrested protesters and drop all charges against them. A deadline of 20 June is set for the government to meet the demands. A fifth frequently expressed demand is that the chief executive and relevant ministers resign.

On 17 June, the police commissioner already qualified the initial blanket characterisation of the 12 June protest as a riot, saying only those who threw bricks or wielded metal poles will be liable for riot, but the Chief Executive has referred to protesters as "blatant rioters". On 19 June, the secretary for security defends police against charges of excessive and inappropriate use of force. On 22 June, the secretary for justice rejects the demand that charges be dropped against protesters, saying the law must run its course.

21 JUNE

Thirty thousand protesters surround police headquarters. Police withdraw to within the compound. Protesters barricade the complex, pelt it with eggs, spray-paint anti-police slogans on the exterior and destroy security cameras.

26 JUNE

Following a rally of 80,000 in nearby Edinburgh Place calling on G20 countries to support Hong Kong protesters at their upcoming summit, 3,000 protesters participate in a second siege of police headquarters. Again, police take no clearance action.

27 & 28 JUNE

"Stand with Hong Kong at G20" ads are published in at least 17 newspapers in 12 countries around the world during the G20 summit in Osaka, Japan. The Freedom Hong Kong publicity campaign crowdfunded over HK$5 million from more than 20,000 donors in a matter of hours on 25 June to pay for the ads.

1 JULY

On the 18th anniversary of the handover, 550,000 march. Another 30,000 contribute to breaking into the Legco building. Several hundred enter it in the late evening, spray-painting slogans and vandalising symbols of state power. From a speech by a protester in the Legco chamber demanding democracy, the fifth and last of the five demands emerges: full and genuine universal suffrage in elections for the chief executive and Legco, the very demand at the heart of the 2014 Umbrella Movement. Protesters retreat before an announced police clearance operation, and none are arrested that night, but in the coming days, police threaten mass arrests.

7 JULY

Two hundred and thirty thousand take part in the first district march in Kowloon. Twelve subsequent district marches occur in July and August in many different districts around the city. At least 1.3 million participate in all. These marches, organised online or by local groups, are a major way of spreading the uprising, and police eventually crack down on them.

9 JULY

A Lennon Wall census shows that 165 Lennon Walls have been built in just about every neighbourhood within the past 10 days. The original Hong Kong Lennon Wall was at government headquarters in the 2014 Umbrella Movement. When protesters surrounded the headquarters on 12 June, they erected a new Lennon Wall. It was destroyed by pro-CCPers on 30 June. Protesters rebuilt it, but when police moved in after the 1 July Legco break-in, it was destroyed again. Many of the new Lennon Walls around Hong Kong are more elaborate than the original and will continue to be maintained for months. Many will also be torn down by pro-CCPers. Eventually, the government will order a coordinated campaign by government workers to tear down the Lennon Walls. Still, some continue to pop up even after that.

14 JULY

One hundred and fifteen thousand take part in the second district march, this one in Sha Tin. Organised by local group Sha Tin Commons, it is the first ever large protest in New Territories, the most populous of Hong Kong's three regions.

21 JULY

Four hundred and thirty thousand take part in a march on Hong Kong Island. For the first time, police place restrictions on a march, ordering it to end in Wan Chai, before reaching the vicinity of government headquarters. Many ignore the order and continue to march past there. Some protesters go to the Central Government Liaison Office, the official headquarters of the PRC government in Hong Kong, which has been left unguarded by police focused on defending Hong Kong government headquarters. The protesters deface the state emblem above the entrance. Apart from the defacing of the HKSAR emblem in Legco on 1 July, this is the protesters' first direct attack on the PRC government. The CCP is furious. A spate of incidents in which PRC flags are torn down from flagpoles and defaced elicits similar condemnation. CCP propaganda against a "separatist" uprising increases.

Later in the evening, more than 100 thugs in white T-shirts attack citizens with metal rods and rattan sticks in Yuen Long. After two police officers on the scene disappear, police take more than half an hour to respond to emergency calls and are then seen chatting amicably with the thugs, leading to accusations of police-thug collusion. Forty-five victims are hospitalised with injuries. No arrests are made that evening, though after an outcry, some three dozen are made in subsequent days and weeks. The event will go down as one of the most infamous and severely damage citizens' trust in the police. After police unions unleash harsh criticism of the chief secretary, the number two government official, when he halfheartedly attempts to apologise for the attacks, he emphasises his full support of police. A top police official later blames protesters for the attacks, claiming that the presence of some provoked the white-shirted thugs. There was no substantial protester presence in the area.

26 JULY

Fifteen thousand participate in an airport sit-in organised by aviation workers, the first of several such protests to take place at the airport in the coming weeks.

27 JULY

Two hundred and eighty-eight thousand take part in a march in Yuen Long against the 21 July thug attacks and police inaction/complicity. The march is banned by police, the very first of altogether 20 marches to be banned over the coming months.

28 JULY

Police ban another march but allow a rally in Chater Garden. Some protesters spread out to nearby streets. Police make 49 arrests in Sheung Wan, not far from the Liaison Office. Forty-four are brought to court on 31 July and charged with riot, the first of three mass trials for riot, and, up to this point, the largest trial in Hong Kong history, soon to be superseded by two others.

3 AUGUST

One hundred and twenty thousand participate in a march in Mong Kok. Protests spread to Tsim Sha Tsui and Wong Tai Sin. The march was originally banned by police but a rally was approved. Upon appeal, a highly truncated march was allowed on a very different route from that first proposed. Protesters deviate from the route and are attacked by police.

4 AUGUST
One hundred and fifty thousand participate in a march in Tseung Kwan O, and 20,000 in a rally in western Hong Kong Island, where police have banned a march.

5 AUGUST
Two hundred and ninety thousand take part in assemblies at seven locations around Hong Kong as part of a general strike of 350,000 workers from 20 sectors, the biggest strike in Hong Kong in living memory. From the early morning, subway lines are suspended and roads are blocked, severely disrupting transport. Two hundred and twenty-four flights are cancelled.

6 AUGUST
At a rare press conference held by the Hong Kong and Macau Affairs Office of the State Council in Beijing, a spokesperson warns, "Those who play with fire will perish by it... Radical protests...are pushing [Hong Kong] into a dangerous abyss. Don't ever misjudge the situation and mistake our restraint for weakness... Don't ever underestimate the firm resolve and immense strength of the central government." Communist Party officials have remained mostly silent regarding the two-month-old crisis in Hong Kong, preferring to give the impression that this is Hong Kong's local problem to solve and they have nothing to do with it, but they are beginning to speak out.

State media distribute a video of 12,000 Chinese police officers staging an anti-riot drill in Shenzhen, just across the border from Hong Kong, claiming the drills are public security measures in preparation for the PRC's seventieth anniversary.

9 - 11 AUGUST
Thousands take part in a three-day airport sit-in. The initial

intention is to bring the plight of Hong Kong people to the attention of international visitors to the city, but as the idea catches on, some begin to see the utility of disrupting international travel to and from Hong Kong.

9 AUGUST
The PRC aviation authority warns Cathay Pacific that staff who have participated in "illegal protests", "violent actions" and "radical activities" will not be allowed to fly in the PRC, where Cathay has extensive operations.

10 & 11 AUGUST
Thousands take part in three banned marches, in Tai Po on 10 August and Sham Shui Po and Hong Kong Island East on 11 August.

12 AUGUST
For the first time, protesters enter the departures hall at the airport, about 5,000 in all. Protests have previously been confined to the arrivals hall. All flights are cancelled.

Following the PRC aviation authority's warning of 9 August, Cathay Pacific warns employees they could be subject to disciplinary measures or fired for supporting or participating in "illegal protests". It subsequently fires employees for their social media posts, including the head of the flight attendants union on 23 August.

CCP mouthpiece *People's Daily* posts a video of armoured military vehicles in Shenzhen at the border with Hong Kong, saying that the People's Armed Police are empowered by law to deal with riots. A spokesperson of the Hong Kong and Macau Affairs Office of the State Council, the organ that's been tasked with releasing the most explicit threats against Hong Kong, says "the first signs of terrorism" are emerging in the Hong Kong protests.

12 - 15 AUGUST
Medical workers stage sit-in protests at 15 hospitals to protest police violence.

13 AUGUST
After flights resume in the morning, protesters fill the airport departures hall again. Some detain two people they suspect of being CCP agents. One is a *Global Times* reporter. Police enter the hall to free them. Flights are cancelled for a second day.

14 AUGUST
The Airport Authority applies for and receives from the High Court an injunction against protests at the airport.

17 AUGUST
State media post a video of the People's Armed Police in Shenzhen conducting training exercises involving mock clashes with protesters.

17 & 18 AUGUST
In conjunction with the 18 August protest in Hong Kong, Stand with Hong Kong solidarity protests are held in at least 37 cities in 12 countries around the world.

18 AUGUST
One million seven hundred thousand take part in a protest on Hong Kong Island. Police banned the planned march but allowed a rally in Victoria Park. There are so many protesters that they fill many of the streets of central Hong Kong Island. This is the third protest of more than one million people.

20 AUGUST

News breaks that a Hong Kong citizen, Simon Cheng, working for the British consulate in Hong Kong, has disappeared in the PRC. On 24 August, Chinese authorities confirm that he was detained and has been released. He returns to Hong Kong. It transpires that he was arrested on 8 August in the part of the express rail terminus in Hong Kong under Chinese jurisdiction as he was attempting to return to Hong Kong. He was brought back to the PRC, where he was forced to confess to soliciting prostitution and held in so-called administrative detention. In November, Cheng, having fled to an unspecified country, says he was tortured during interrogation to force him to confess to inciting protesters to violence on behalf of the UK. His horrible story represents everything Hong Kong protesters are fighting against in the extradition bill.

23 AUGUST

Two hundred and ten thousand participate in the Hong Kong Way, a series of human chains stretching across many parts of Hong Kong and modelled after the Baltic Way, which took place on this date in 1989, when millions held hands in Estonia, Latvia and Lithuania along the Russian border to protest for freedom and independence. It inspires hundreds of smaller human chains in the weeks to come.

24 AUGUST

Tens of thousands take part in a march in Kwun Tong. Though the march is approved by the police, MTR closes four stations in the vicinity. This is the beginning of MTR closing stations to make it more difficult for protesters to attend protests, even authorised ones. In coming days and weeks, some protesters retaliate by vandalising MTR stations. MTR reacts by closing more stations. A vicious cycle ensues. Like Cathay Pacific, MTR is perceived by protesters as a company that is doing the political bidding of the Party. It also has extensive business interests in the PRC. Unlike Cathay, MTR is 75 per cent government-owned, and its services are central to Hong Kong's transport network. Both Cathay and MTR have in the past been regarded by Hong Kong people with pride as symbols of Hong Kong's efficiency and high quality. Their hijacking by the Party is regarded as indicative of what already happens in the PRC, where companies are routinely required to do the Party's bidding, and an omen of what will happen if people don't prevent it.

29 AUGUST

State media post yet another video of the People's Armed Police in Shenzhen conducting anti-riot drills. After this, explicit and implicit threats taper off as the Party appears to realise that it's not scaring Hong Kong protesters but raising alarm in the rest of the world, and the longer they go on without action, the less effective they will be.

29 & 30 AUGUST

Ahead of a 31 August march banned by police, nine pro-democracy leaders are arrested on various charges related to various protests in June and July.

31 AUGUST

Tens of thousands defy the ban and march on Hong Kong Island. Police storm Prince Edward MTR station, beating passengers with batons and pepper-spraying them. This incident becomes nearly as notorious as the 21 July thug attacks in Yuen Long. Police stonewall investigation, and the MTR refuses to release full security camera footage to the public.

2 SEPTEMBER

Tens of thousands participate in a coordinated general strike of workers and a class boycott by university and secondary students.

2 - 30 SEPTEMBER

On 2 September, the first secondary student human chain protests are held. Over the coming month, tens of thousands of students from at least 343 secondary schools will take part in human chain protests. On 9 September alone, students from 188 schools form human chains; on 12 September, 47; and on eight other days in September, anywhere between three and 20.

4 SEPTEMBER

Chief executive Carrie Lam announces that the extradition bill will be fully withdrawn when Legco reopens in October. This fulfils one of the protests' five demands, the only one to be met. The announcement is perceived as too little too late and has almost no effect on the protests. The timing of the announcement is likely determined by the CCP's hope that the Hong Kong protests will end before its 1 October celebrations of the seventieth anniversary of the PRC.

8 SEPTEMBER

Two hundred and fifty thousand attend a police-approved march to the US consulate to call on the US to pass the Hong Kong Human Rights and Democracy Act. The police terminate the march and attack protesters after some protesters vandalise nearby MTR station entrances. This becomes the last march police will approve until 1 December.

8 SEPTEMBER - 1 DECEMBER

Police ban all marches. Their justification is that the probability of violence and other unlawful activity is high. In all, six applications for marches are rejected in this period. Other organisers don't even bother to apply. Police try to prevent and attack at least nine protests in this period.

9 - 12 SEPTEMBER

On 31 August, the song "Glory to Hong Kong" is published on YouTube. From 9 to 12 September, at least 22 "Glory to Hong Kong" sing-along protests are held at shopping malls. "Glory to Hong Kong" quickly becomes recognised among protesters as the new Hong Kong national anthem. This is also the beginning of a trend of shopping malls becoming frequent sites of protest, considered safer at a time when police are attacking just about every protest and all marches are banned. In the coming period, some protesters begin to vandalise perceived pro-Communist shops in malls, and police start entering malls in pursuit.

14 SEPTEMBER

Freedom Hong Kong crowdfunds HK$8.3 million (US$1.1million) in a matter of a few hours to publish advertisements in dozens of countries and languages around the world on 1 October, the anniversary of the PRC and thus CCP dictatorship. The ads will give the Hong Kong perspective on that anniversary. This is its second successful global advertising campaign after Stand with Hong Kong at G20 on 27 and 28 June.

15 SEPTEMBER

Four hundred and ninety thousand attend a banned march from Causeway Bay to Central.

28 SEPTEMBER

Two hundred thousand attend a rally in Tamar Park commemorating the fifth anniversary of the start of the Umbrella Movement.

29 SEPTEMBER

Solidarity protests in at least 72 cities in 20 countries mark Global Anti-Totalitarianism Day. In Hong Kong, police try to prevent a march whose organisers refused to apply for permission by attacking it with tear gas, but 200,000 march in defiance. Many protesters are arrested. On 2 October, 96 are charged in court with riot, surpassing the trial of 44 for riot that began on 31 July as the largest trial in Hong Kong history. The defendants include doctors, nurses, teachers, surveyors, social workers and many students.

1 OCTOBER

In Beijing, the largest military parade in PRC history marks the 17th anniversary of CCP dictatorship. In Hong Kong, protesters declare a "day of mourning"; 200,000 take part in a banned march from Causeway Bay to Central. Protests take place in at least 13 locations around Hong Kong, including Yau Ma Tei, Mong Kok, Prince Edward, Sham Shui Po, Wong Tai Sin, Tsuen Wan, Tuen Mun and Sha Tin. Police attack most of them. A total of 269 people are arrested; the police fire 1,400 tear gas canisters, 900 rubber bullets, 190 beanbag rounds and 230 sponge grenades, record numbers in a single day. Six live rounds are fired. In the late afternoon, a police officer shoots an 18-year-old in the chest at point-blank range. Miraculously, he survives. He is later charged with riot and assaulting police.

4 OCTOBER

Chief executive Carrie Lam announces a ban on face masks effective 5 October. The ban prohibits all facial coverings at public gatherings. The Emergency Regulations Ordinance, enacted in the 1920s, is invoked in order to declare the ban by fiat, without any legislative process. The government appears to believe the mask ban will dissuade protesters from coming out, but it has the opposite effect.

In the evening, protests against the ban take place in a dozen areas of Hong Kong. One of the main slogans of the protests so far, "Hong Kong people, persist!" (香港人加油)) is transformed into

"Hong Kong people, resist!" (香港人反抗).

In Yuen Long, an off-duty police officer shoots a 14-year-old boy in the left thigh at close range. This is the second police gunshot victim. He is arrested and charged with riot on 5 October.

In the late evening, MTR suspends all operations until further notice. The following day, dozens of shopping malls are closed.

6 OCTOBER

Six hundred and fifty thousand take part in an unauthorised march from Causeway Bay to Central. One hundred and fifty thousand take part in an unauthorised march in central Kowloon. Both marches are against the face mask ban. Many smaller protests occur in the vicinity of the marches.

11 OCTOBER

MTR reopens all its stations after being shut for nearly a week. Legco holds its first session after extensive repairs necessitated by the damage caused by the 1 July break-in.

14 OCTOBER

One hundred and thirty thousand rally at Chater Garden to call on the US to pass the Hong Kong Human Rights and Democracy Act.

20 OCTOBER

Three hundred and fifty thousand take part in a banned march in central Kowloon.

23 OCTOBER

Confessed murderer Chan Tong-kai is released from prison after having served 21 months of his 29-month sentence for money laundering.

Legco formally withdraws the extradition bill that sparked the protests. The chief executive had announced on 4 September that the bill would be withdrawn.

29 OCTOBER
Pro-democracy icon Joshua Wong is the first and ultimately only candidate to be barred from running in 24 November District Council elections, on grounds that he belongs to a political party that advocates self-determination. Since Legco elections in 2016, more than a dozen candidates have been disqualified on political grounds.

2 NOVEMBER
Three hundred thousand take part in a Fight for Autonomy rally in Victoria Park that police banned. Participants tried to circumvent the ban by designating it an election meeting, but although the gathering is peaceful, blocking no roads, and entirely within a public park, police attack it with tear gas. Protests spread to various locations in central Hong Kong Island.

4 NOVEMBER
Twenty-two-year-old Chow Tsz-lok falls in Sheung Tak car park in Tseung Kwan O, where police are conducting a clearance operation. Suspicion falls on police but they deny any involvement. He is unconscious from the moment he is discovered and never regains consciousness. Link REIT, the owner of the car park, releases full security camera footage to the public. None of it shows Chow's fall.

8 NOVEMBER
Chow Tsz-lok dies. Vigils are held for him at 10 locations around the city. Ten thousand gather at the spot where he fell.

9 NOVEMBER
Seven pro-democracy Legco members are arrested in relation to an altercation in Legco over the extradition bill way back in May. The arrests echo the arrests of nine pro-democracy leaders on 29 and 30 August and come just before major protest actions called to start 11 November and District Council elections on 24 November, which the government is rumoured to be considering postponing or cancelling.

One hundred thousand mourn Chow Tsz-lok at a gathering held in Tamar Park.

11 NOVEMBER
In response to the death of Chow Tsz-lok, protest actions labelled Operation Dawn and called to last a week, kicking off with transport disruptions that nearly paralyse the city and the suspension of classes at 11 universities. Police enter the campuses of three universities, including two they will later besiege, Chinese University of Hong Kong and Polytechnic University, leading to clashes with protesters. In Sai Wan Ho, a police officer shoots a 21-year-old in the stomach at point-blank range. The victim is in critical condition but eventually survives. This is the third police gunshot victim. All three were shot at close range.

Lunchtime protests are held in Central and Mong Kok, where 10,000 and 5,000 gather, respectively. Many office workers join during their lunch break. These are the first of at least 82 lunchtime protests that will be held in at least 13 locations over the coming weeks, including Tai Koo, Wong Chuk Hang, Kwun Tong, Kowloon Bay, Cheung Sha Wan, Kwai Chung, San Po Kong, Causeway Bay, Wan Chai, Tsim Sha Tsui and Sha Tin.

12 & 13 NOVEMBER
Protesters lay roadblocks in at least 13 districts of the city. Starting

in the afternoon of the 12th, police besiege CUHK until late into the night of the 13th. The stand-off centres on a bridge. Police fire hundreds of rounds of tear gas and rubber bullets. Protesters respond with petrol bombs and bricks and set fires to impede police offensives. At times, the conflict resembles war. More than 100 students are injured.

13 NOVEMBER

For the third straight day, much of the transport network is paralysed. Further barricades and roadblocks are erected around Hong Kong, while the campuses of PolyU, University of Hong Kong, CUHK, Baptist University and City University are fortified against police attack.

In the evening, a 15-year-old boy is hit in the head by a tear gas canister in Tin Shui Wai. He undergoes brain surgery. His is the fourth near-fatality caused by police projectiles. He will remain in a coma for more than a month, awakening on 21 December. Even then, his prospects for recovery remain uncertain.

17 - 29 NOVEMBER

Police begin to lay siege to PolyU. By late evening, they have surrounded the whole campus and cordoned it off. They threaten to storm it using lethal force. Hundreds are trapped inside. The siege will last for a total of 12 days, with hundreds arrested and hundreds of others escaping by abseiling from a bridge, going through the sewer system and other means.

18 NOVEMBER

Fifty-five thousand protesters in several areas near PolyU attempt to break the police siege but are repeatedly beaten back. By evening, police go on the offensive, conducting mass arrests. On 20 November, 213 of those arrested are charged with riot in six courthouses around the city. This is the largest trial in Hong Kong history, surpassing the trial of 96 for riot that started on 2 October.

The High Court rules the Hong Kong government ban on face masks at protests is unconstitutional. The government later announces it will appeal the ruling. Whatever the outcome, the face mask ban has had virtually no effect on people wearing masks at protests and is perceived as simply another way the regime is stripping away people's civil liberties.

24 NOVEMBER

Pro-democracy candidates win a landslide victory in District Council elections, capturing 389 of 452 seats and gaining control of 17 of the 18 District Councils. The turnout of over 71 per cent is a record in any election ever held in Hong Kong. The result shows overwhelming majority support for the protests and condemnation of the government and police.

27 NOVEMBER

The US president signs the Hong Kong Human Rights and Democracy Act and the PROTECT Hong Kong Act into law. This is the first concrete step taken by a foreign government in support of the Hong Kong protests.

28 NOVEMBER

One hundred thousand gather in Edinburgh Place to hold a rally of Thanksgiving to the US for passing the Hong Kong Human Rights and Democracy Act and the PROTECT Hong Kong Act.

1 DECEMBER

Three hundred and eighty thousand people march from Tsim Sha Tsui to Hung Hom in the first authorised march since 8 September. In spite of having approved the march, police attack marchers with tear gas. Clashes later ensue in Tsim Sha Tsui, Whampoa and Mong Kok.

8 DECEMBER

Eight hundred thousand take part in a march from Victoria Park to Central organised by Civil Human Rights Front. It is the first protest of any kind organised by the non-violent CHRF to be approved by police since 17 August, when a rally was approved but a march banned. The protest marks six months since the start of the protests on 9 June and International Human Rights Day on 10 December. Its purpose is to advocate for democracy and human rights in Hong Kong.

19 DECEMBER

Hong Kong police freeze more than HK$70 million belonging to Spark Alliance and arrest four members of the group for money laundering. The money was donated by ordinary Hong Kong people to a fund to help arrested, prosecuted and injured protesters. The police actions are interpreted as an attempt to crack down on the movement by going after its funding, which is substantial. In all, various groups assisting protesters have raised more than HK$200 million, with 612 Humanitarian Relief Fund and Spark Alliance being the biggest.

2020

1 JANUARY

About 1.03 million people march from Victoria Park to Central in the fourth protest of more than one million. Though the march is approved and almost entirely peaceful, police attack protesters and terminate the march, arresting hundreds.

19 JANUARY

One hundred and fifty thousand attend a Universal Siege of Communism rally in Chater Garden and Chater Road. The rally organiser originally applied for permission for a march, but that was denied. Though the rally was approved and almost entirely peaceful, police attack protesters, tear-gas and terminate the rally, and arrest the rally organiser.

21 - 25 JANUARY
After the government bans stalls selling dry goods (as opposed to flowers) at Chinese New Year fairs it runs to prevent political groups from having stalls, about a dozen pro-democracy New Year fairs are set up across the city. They sell protest-themed merchandise and promote pro-democracy causes.

23 JANUARY
The first protest is held against the government handling of the coronavirus, in particular its refusal to take adequate precautions to prevent the spread of the coronavirus from the PRC. In the next month, at least 38 coronavirus-related protests are held, most calling for the closure of the border with the PRC or opposing government designation of particular sites as coronavirus quarantine centres or treatment clinics without sufficient participation of the community in decision making.

25 JANUARY
Chief executive Carrie Lam declares the coronavirus outbreak an emergency but refuses to close the border with the PRC despite many health experts and 80 per cent of Hong Kong people advocating border closure. She says it would be "inappropriate and impractical", later adding it would be "discriminatory" and "stigmatising" and would go against World Health Organization recommendations that travel restrictions not be imposed. A month later, on 24 February, the government announces it will bar arrivals from South Korea (except for Hong Kong residents).

28 JANUARY

The Hospital Authority Employees Alliance, one of the at least 135 new pro-democracy unions formed since June 2019, announces that 15,000 members have now joined and threatens to go on strike if the government doesn't close the border with the PRC and ensure adequate provisions for front-line medical personnel and patients.

3 FEBRUARY

An initial five-day strike of Hospital Authority workers begins with a "soft strike" of non-emergency workers. On 4 February, all other striking workers join in, approximately 7,000 in all. Along with protests and diverse civil society groups, the strike pressures the government to take additional measures to fight the coronavirus epidemic and avoid its spread in Hong Kong, including the closure of all ports of entry from the PRC except the airport and two overland crossings. It is not the full border closure most have demanded, but it is better than before. Arrivals from the PRC drop significantly in coming days. At the end of the week, workers vote to return to work.

29 MARCH

The Hong Kong government imposes pandemic prevention measures that include a ban on all public gatherings of more than four people. For the next 33 months – nearly three years – the ban will remain in place (at various times limiting the maximum size of a public gathering to two, four, eight and 50 people), with the right to freedom of assembly indefinitely suspended. During that period, there were major protests of hundreds of thousands in the US, Sudan, Belarus, India, France, Russia, Myanmar and other countries without any evidence that such outdoor public gatherings contributed to the spread of the coronavirus. After the ban on public gatherings was finally lifted on 28 December 2022, police continued to impose a variety of arbitrary restrictions to prevent protests.

30 MARCH - 6 JULY
Despite the ban, 105 protests are held in these months, including four protests of more than 150,000.

30 JUNE
At 11pm, the Law of the People's Republic of China on Safeguarding National Security in the Hong Kong Special Administrative Region (commonly referred to as the "national security law") goes into effect. It is imposed on Hong Kong by the Chinese Communist Party without any involvement by anyone in Hong Kong. It outlaws subversion, collusion with foreign forces, secession and terrorism. It creates a new National Security Department within the Hong Kong Police Force and an Office for Safeguarding National Security made up of Chinese government officials located in Hong Kong to administer the law. Hong Kong has no jurisdiction over the office and it is entirely secret. In practice, the draconian edict is used by the authorities to crush any and all forms of dissent and becomes one of the regime's most important tools in transforming Hong Kong into an authoritarian society.

1 JULY
On the first full day the national security law (NSL) is in effect, 150,000 protest against it, even though the protest is banned and attacked by police; 370 people are arrested, including 10 for violating the NSL. One year later, on 30 July 2021, one of those 10 is sentenced to nine years in prison after being convicted of "terrorism" and "inciting secession" for skidding into a group of police officers on his motorcycle while flying a "liberate Hong Kong, revolution of our times" flag.

Brian Kern is a writer and activist. He has written two books on Hong Kong, *Umbrella: A Political Tale from Hong Kong* and *As long as there is resistance, there is hope: Essays on the Hong Kong freedom struggle in the post-Umbrella Movement era, 2014-2018*, under the pseudonym Kong Tsung-gan.